Practical Game Design with Unity and Playmaker

Leverage the power of Unity 3D and Playmaker to develop a game from scratch

Sergey Mohov

BIRMINGHAM - MUMBAI

Practical Game Design with Unity and Playmaker

Copyright © 2013 Packt Publishing

All rights reserved. No part of this book may be reproduced, stored in a retrieval system, or transmitted in any form or by any means, without the prior written permission of the publisher, except in the case of brief quotations embedded in critical articles or reviews.

Every effort has been made in the preparation of this book to ensure the accuracy of the information presented. However, the information contained in this book is sold without warranty, either express or implied. Neither the authors, nor Packt Publishing, and its dealers and distributors will be held liable for any damages caused or alleged to be caused directly or indirectly by this book.

Packt Publishing has endeavored to provide trademark information about all of the companies and products mentioned in this book by the appropriate use of capitals. However, Packt Publishing cannot guarantee the accuracy of this information.

First published: December 2013

Production Reference: 1131213

Published by Packt Publishing Ltd.
Livery Place
35 Livery Street
Birmingham B3 2PB, UK.

ISBN 978-1-84969-810-8

www.packtpub.com

Cover Image by Asif Khan (asifmuradkhan@gmail.com)

Credits

Author
Sergey Mohov

Reviewers
Sangram Dange
Philip 'MrPhil' Ludington
Pedro Machado Santa
Callan Winfield

Acquisition Editors
Meeta Rajani
Vinay Argekar

Lead Technical Editor
Ruchita Bhansali

Technical Editors
Tanvi Bhatt
Shiny Poojary
Faisal Siddiqui

Project Coordinator
Jomin Varghese

Proofreader
Lawrence A. Herman

Indexer
Tejal Soni

Graphics
Yuvraj Mannari

Production Coordinator
Saiprasad Kadam

Cover Work
Saiprasad Kadam

About the Author

Sergey Mohov is a game developer and designer with over three years of experience in working on games in Unity. His prominent projects include Dédale, Paradis Perdus, and Lune. The rest of Sergey's games can be found on his website at `http://sergeymohov.com` along with his personal blog.

> I would like to thank everyone in the Unity community who helped me get from nothing to something. Special thanks to Mike Renwick who leaves no question unanswered. Many thanks to my friends and family for your continuing support. Thanks to Gwen, because everyone needs to get distracted every now and then.
>
> I can't go without thanking the staff at Packt Publishing for suggesting that I write this book and for their guidance throughout the process.

About the Reviewers

Philip 'MrPhil' Ludington grew up on the Gulf Coast of Mississippi, in the small city of Pascagoula, enthralled with computers and video games. He first learned to program as a young boy reading the BASIC manual that came with the family's first computer, a TI-99/4A. Working his way through college driving 40 ft. buses, he earned a Bachelor of Science degree from the University of Maryland at College Park. After more than 15 years as a programmer, he has worked at some recognizable companies including AT&T and SAP, in a range of industries from government contracting to education and casino gaming. In his spare time, Philip enjoys alpine skiing, playing board games with friends, and making video games for his website, www.MrPhilGames.com. Philip is currently working on a game about building railroads called Iron Roads.

Pedro Machado Santa is a 29-year-old Portuguese digital crafter and relentless hacker who has a software engineer title in his diploma. He holds a Masters degree in Informatics Engineering from the University of Coimbra and was an R&D research grant holder in 2011 at Instituto Pedro Nunes working in the fields of design science research, augmented reality, interaction design, and game authoring tools.

He previously worked as a mobile game designer and developer at HumanSpot (`http://www.humanspot.com`), a small technology and media services company based in Coimbra, Portugal. Currently he is based in the United Arab Emirates working at Sports Stars Media (SSM, `http://www.sportsstarsmedia.com`) where he participated as game designer and Unity3D developer on the official mobile soccer game and augmented reality app for the Mourinho and The Special Ones franchise. He continues to perform both as a web and mobile developer for other present and future SSM projects.

> I can't go without thanking Paula for her relentless support and encouragement in all my projects, to my Sports Stars Media teammates Joel and José for the exciting and sincere enthusiasm they always showed during our lengthy discussions about the best Unity3D solutions and strategies, to Sergey for heartily attending to all my comments, and to all the nice staff at Packt Publishing, especially to Jomin and Aurita for the invitation to review this book.

www.PacktPub.com

Support files, eBooks, discount offers and more

You might want to visit www.PacktPub.com for support files and downloads related to your book.

Did you know that Packt offers eBook versions of every book published, with PDF and ePub files available? You can upgrade to the eBook version at www.PacktPub.com and as a print book customer, you are entitled to a discount on the eBook copy. Get in touch with us at service@packtpub.com for more details.

At www.PacktPub.com, you can also read a collection of free technical articles, sign up for a range of free newsletters and receive exclusive discounts and offers on Packt books and eBooks.

http://PacktLib.PacktPub.com

Do you need instant solutions to your IT questions? PacktLib is Packt's online digital book library. Here, you can access, read and search across Packt's entire library of books.

Why Subscribe?

- Fully searchable across every book published by Packt
- Copy and paste, print and bookmark content
- On demand and accessible via web browser

Free Access for Packt account holders

If you have an account with Packt at www.PacktPub.com, you can use this to access PacktLib today and view nine entirely free books. Simply use your login credentials for immediate access.

Table of Contents

Preface   1

Chapter 1: Getting Started with Unity and Playmaker   7
- **Downloading and installing Unity**   7
- **Buying and importing Playmaker**   11
- **Setting up your project**   13
- **Summary**   17

Chapter 2: Unity's and Playmaker's User Interface   19
- **Interface overview and main menu**   19
  - Hierarchy panel   23
  - Inspector panel   25
  - Project panel   28
  - Views   29
- **Playmaker interface**   32
- **Summary**   34

Chapter 3: Components and State Machines   35
- **Game objects, components, and properties**   35
- **Working with prefabs**   39
- **Finite state machines, states, and actions**   43
- **Interaction between game objects**   47
- **Summary**   50

Chapter 4: Creating Your First Game   51
- **Using Vector geometry and physics**   51
- **Win or lose conditions**   55
- **Creating artificial intelligence**   60
- **Exercises**   67
- **Summary**   69

Table of Contents

Chapter 5: Scripting and Custom Actions	**71**
Writing a Unity Script	71
Overview of standard Unity classes	75
Creating a Playmaker action	77
Summary	82
Chapter 6: Networking and Multiplayer	**83**
Understanding networking and multiplayer	83
Setting up Photon Unity Networking	86
Making multiplayer	88
Summary	96
Chapter 7: Working with External APIs	**97**
About external application programming interfaces	97
Uploading your game to Kongregate	98
Writing Kongregate API code	99
Summary	104
Index	**105**

Preface

Historically, game design has been a broad term. It is still often associated uniquely with creating the rules of a game, establishing a system, defining what the game will be in broad brushstrokes and then creating particular gameplay scenarios or levels. Sometimes, we go a little farther and endow game designers with the power to define how the game's universe and aesthetics will work. Broad as this definition might seem, it remains very limited in one area, and that is technology.

As the game industry moves toward its maturation, many small studios begin to emerge, often teams of one, two, or three individuals, attributing their success to the new generation of tools now available to game developers. While the larger game companies employing hundreds of developers have mostly been able to stand their ground, in this new landscape, the focus has already shifted toward polyvalence and self-sufficiency.

Game designers have always wanted more control over the games that they make, and, for the first time in history, there is no reason why they should not reach out and take it. Knowing how your game works on the inside means having more control and creative freedom. It also means more effective communication with other members of the team, provided there are any. It empowers you to go ahead and simply make the game on your own, be it a mere prototype, a game jam project, or a full commercial release.

Unity 3D is a game authoring tool that has changed the way we think about game development forever, making it much cheaper and more democratic. It allows anyone willing to invest their time into it to craft amazing game worlds and experiences for next to nothing. It has been one of the major forces driving this incredible change, with millions of new developers joining the game industry simply because they can now. The industry becomes more open every day, which enriches the pool of ideas that people bring to it from different backgrounds.

Preface

This book is an introduction to practical game design using Unity and Playmaker by Hutong Games. The latter lets anyone make a game without writing any programming code, while not giving up any of the power that Unity has to offer. Knowing the basics of programming is still valuable while working on the technical side of a game, but going deep into it is no longer an imperative, which means that creating a game is now easier than it has ever been before.

Even if you know how to code, learning how to use Playmaker in Unity may help you see the synergy between your game's mechanics and technology more clearly, making the development of your project more about finding the right design and less about working around the computer code.

There can be no doubt about the bright future of the practical aspect of game design, and this book offers you to become part of this future.

What this book covers

Chapter 1, Getting Started with Unity and Playmaker, gives us information about installing Unity, buying and installing Playmaker, creating and setting up the project, and making some adjustments to the interface layout.

Chapter 2, Unity's and Playmaker's User Interface, gives an introduction to the essential interface elements of Unity and Playmaker: menus, panels, and views.

Chapter 3, Components and State Machines, gives details about the project structure in Unity with and without Playmaker and introduces the component-based approach to game development.

Chapter 4, Creating Your First Game, gives information about applying and expanding your Unity and Playmaker skills learned in previous chapters to create real game mechanics.

Chapter 5, Scripting and Custom Actions, gives an introduction to Unity scripting in JavaScript and C#, making a custom Playmaker action.

Chapter 6, Networking and Multiplayer, gives details about adding multiplayer to your game using the plugin called Photon Cloud.

Chapter 7, Working with External APIs, gives information on working with external APIs, making your game available online on Kongregate, and integrating its online leaderboard.

What you need for this book

You need Windows XP SP2 or later, Windows 7 SP1, or Mac OS X "Snow Leopard" 10.6 or later. Your graphics card must support DirectX 9 with 2.0 shader model.

Playmaker is a paid plugin, so you need to either buy it before beginning to use the book or get it at the Asset Store as explained in *Chapter 1, Getting Started with Unity and Playmaker*.

While not a requirement for the first four chapters, you must have an internet connection in order to be able to integrate multiplayer and external APIs.

Who this book is for

This book is for both new and experienced game designers willing to have more control over the technical side of their games. It is also for people who want a quick comprehensive guide to Unity and Playmaker that allows learning these tools from scratch.

You need to be comfortable enough using your operating system and standard software for it in order to be equally comfortable using Unity. While knowing the basics of programming (such as functions, variables, and values) is important to follow all of the steps in this book (specifically *Chapter 5, Scripting and Custom Actions*), this book provides links to free online resources that will help you learn these concepts quickly and efficiently.

Conventions

In this book, you will find a number of styles of text that distinguish between different kinds of information. Here are some examples of these styles, and an explanation of their meaning.

Code words in text are shown as follows: "You already have the `unitypackage` file with it on your hard drive."

New terms and **important words** are shown in bold. Words that you see on the screen, in menus or dialog boxes for example, appear in the text like this: "Just click the blue **Download** button."

> Warnings or important notes appear in a box like this.

> Tips and tricks appear like this.

Reader feedback

Feedback from our readers is always welcome. Let us know what you think about this book—what you liked or may have disliked. Reader feedback is important for us to develop titles that you really get the most out of.

To send us general feedback, simply send an e-mail to `feedback@packtpub.com`, and mention the book title via the subject of your message. If there is a topic that you have expertise in and you are interested in either writing or contributing to a book, see our author guide on `www.packtpub.com/authors`.

Customer support

Now that you are the proud owner of a Packt book, we have a number of things to help you to get the most from your purchase.

Downloading the example code

You can download the example code files for all Packt books you have purchased from your account at `http://www.packtpub.com`. If you purchased this book elsewhere, you can visit `http://www.packtpub.com/support` and register to have the files e-mailed directly to you.

Errata

Although we have taken every care to ensure the accuracy of our content, mistakes do happen. If you find a mistake in one of our books—maybe a mistake in the text or the code—we would be grateful if you would report this to us. By doing so, you can save other readers from frustration and help us improve subsequent versions of this book. If you find any errata, please report them by visiting http://www.packtpub.com/submit-errata, selecting your book, clicking on the **errata submission form** link, and entering the details of your errata. Once your errata are verified, your submission will be accepted and the errata will be uploaded on our website, or added to any list of existing errata, under the Errata section of that title. Any existing errata can be viewed by selecting your title from http://www.packtpub.com/support.

Piracy

Piracy of copyright material on the Internet is an ongoing problem across all media. At Packt, we take the protection of our copyright and licenses very seriously. If you come across any illegal copies of our works, in any form, on the Internet, please provide us with the location address or website name immediately so that we can pursue a remedy.

Please contact us at copyright@packtpub.com with a link to the suspected pirated material.

We appreciate your help in protecting our authors, and our ability to bring you valuable content.

Questions

You can contact us at questions@packtpub.com if you are having a problem with any aspect of the book, and we will do our best to address it.

1
Getting Started with Unity and Playmaker

In this chapter, we are going to go through the process of getting the project ready to work with this book. We will cover the following subjects:

- Downloading, installing, and setting up Unity
- Buying and installing Playmaker using the Asset Store
- Creating a new project and changing project settings

If you are familiar with the process of downloading and installing Unity and plugins for it, you can move to the section of this chapter called *Setting up your project*. It shows the layout of Unity and project settings that are going to be used for examples in this book.

Downloading and installing Unity

Unity is available for both Mac OS X and Windows PC, and the process of installation for these platforms is very similar. This book is going to use the Mac version of Unity, but I will provide you with alternative directions and hotkeys when they are different in the Windows version. Luckily, everything is, in fact, quite similar, and you should not have any problems switching between the two platforms if you choose to do so.

First things first, let us head over to `http://unity3d.com/unity/download/` and download the latest version of Unity available (as of writing this book the version is 4.3). Just click the blue **Download** button, and the file should start being downloaded to your hard drive. The file in question will be a DMG file for Mac users or an installer EXE for Windows users. Save it wherever you want on your hard drive.

If you are on a Mac, double-clicking the DMG file will reveal the PKG file, which is the installer. Double-clicking Unity.pkg will produce essentially the same result as double-clicking Unity.exe in Windows—it will prompt the installation wizard. You are not given any Unity-specific options except for the location where you want to install the engine.

You can install multiple versions of Unity on the same computer. To do this, you just have to change the name of the folder in which Unity is being installed and put the new installation into a different folder. You might want to do this if you want to have different versions installed at the same time, either because of license restrictions or because of some version-specific features that you want to access. Keep in mind that if you update a project to a newer version of Unity, you cannot go back to an older one.

The following screenshot shows the installation window of Unity. In this stage of the wizard you can specify the directory where Unity will be installed or change some installation parameters. In most cases you will want to install Unity with the default parameters. If that is the case, simply click on **Install** and skip the next step.

If you want to change the install location, click on **Change Install Location....**. The **Customize** button lets you include or exclude specific packages, such as the main Unity installation, example project, and Unity Web Player. Leave all of the boxes checked for this installation. We will talk about packages later in the book.

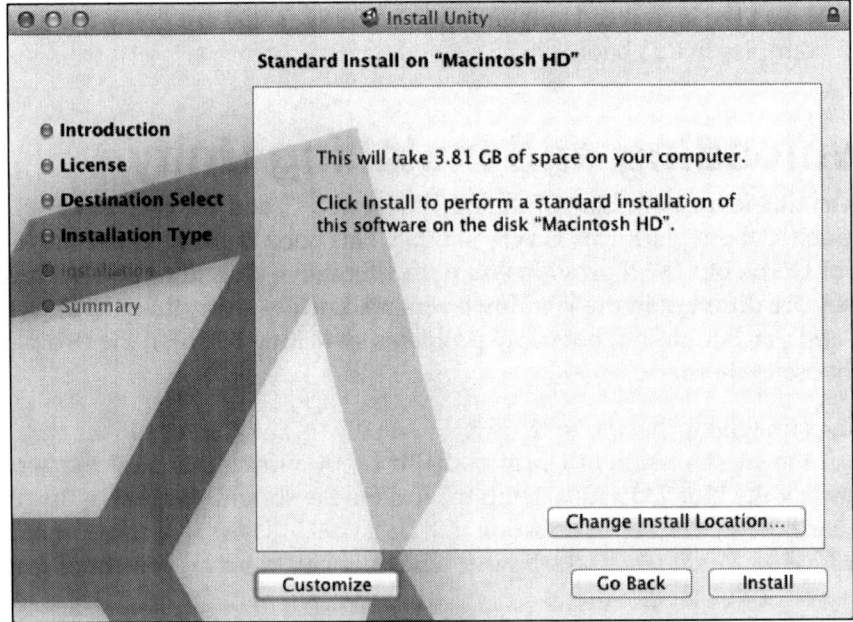

Clicking on **Install** will lead to installation of Unity on your hard drive. Once installation is done, you can go to the folder where you installed it (by default, `Applications/Unity` on Mac or `C:\\Program Files\Unity` in Windows) and launch it.

If you are launching Unity for the first time, a window will pop up asking you to select your type of license and enter your Unity account login and password. Do create an account if you do not have one and enter the details. Later you will need it for things like forum access and Unity answers—both very helpful when you are looking for solutions to Unity-related problems. In this book we are going to be using the free version of Unity, since none of the examples here will require any pro-license features. So select **Activate the free version of Unity** and click on **OK**.

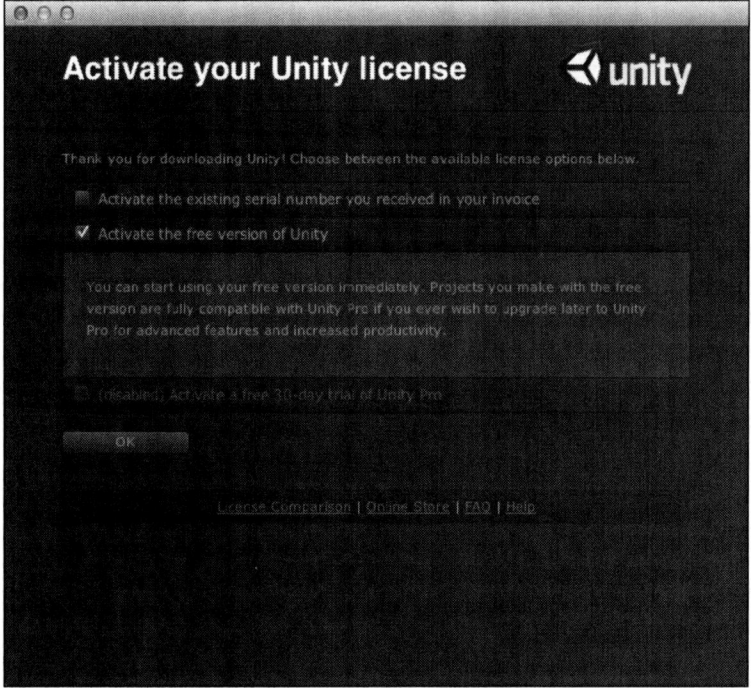

The first time you open Unity, a default project will likely be loaded. These test projects included with the installation (and available through Unity's website) will be quite helpful later on when you want to find out how to do some specific thing (for example, mini-map or water physics), but do not know where to start.

Getting Started with Unity and Playmaker

For now, though, we want a new empty project. Once Unity is loaded, go to the **File** menu in the main menu on the top-left corner of the screen and select **New Project...**.

This will prompt the **Project Wizard** window, in which you can choose where you want your future project to be located, as well as how it will be called. In Unity, a project is a folder, so the name that you give to your project folder will automatically be assigned to the project. For the examples in this book, you will not need any packages at this point, so leave all the checkboxes empty, unless you already have Playmaker downloaded, in which case check Playmaker. When you are ready, click on **Create Project**.

If you want to always start from the **Project Wizard** (which is highly recommended if you are planning to have multiple projects), go to **Unity | Preferences** and check **Always Show Project Wizard**, then close the **Preferences** window. For Windows users it is **File | Preferences** instead.

Since we are not loading any heavy asset packages, the project will load really quickly, and you should see the main Unity interface again, except this time everything will be empty.

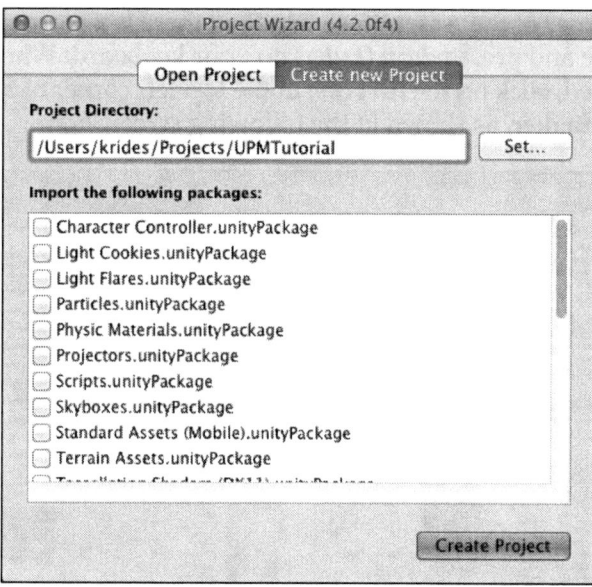

Buying and importing Playmaker

Before we change anything in the layout of our project, there is one missing component that we have to import, which is Playmaker by Hutong Games (http://www.hutonggames.com/)—the main tool (apart from Unity itself) that we are going to be using in most of the exercises in this book. To get Playmaker, we are going to use the Asset Store. The latter is an online market place valuable for any Unity developer, allowing us to save a lot of time by importing useful plugins and asset packs made by other users into our own projects. Some of the assets available through the Asset Store are free, but most of them, like Playmaker, are user-made and cost money. You too can make your tools and assets available through the Asset Store. Think of it as a developer-targeted analogue of the iTunes Store or Amazon.

Although you can access and search the Asset Store through a web page (http://unity3d.com/asset-store/), it is integrated directly into the engine in its most practical form. To access the Asset Store directly from Unity, go to the **Window** submenu in the main menu and select **Asset Store** from the list. This will open the **Asset Store** window in Unity (you need to be connected to the Internet to see the content of the store).

Getting Started with Unity and Playmaker

In the top-right corner of the **Asset Store** window, there is a search box. Type `Playmaker` in there and press *return* (*Enter*) on your keyboard. When the search results are displayed, click on the first one in the top-left corner of **Search Results**, simply called **Playmaker**, as shown in the following screenshot:

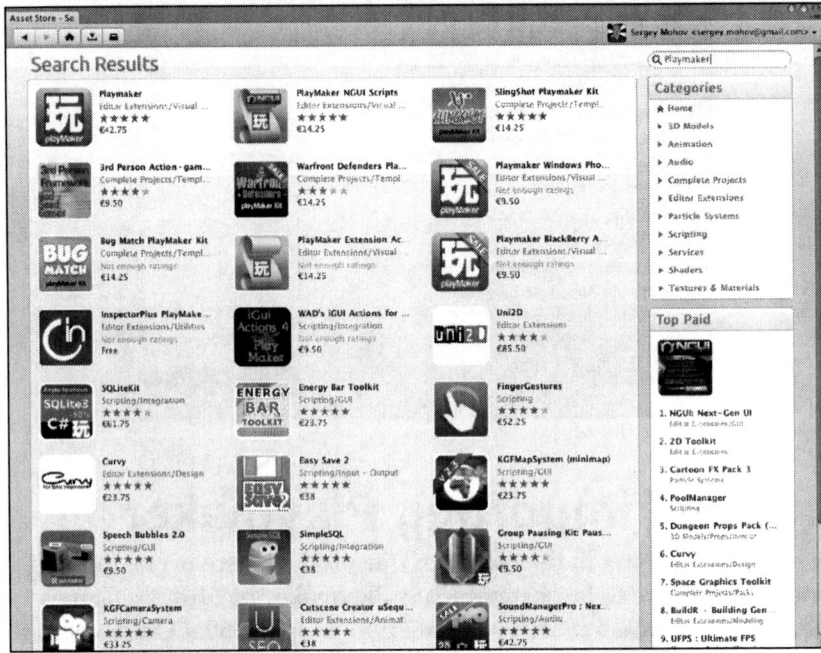

The **Asset Store** window will now display the description of Playmaker, user comments, some screenshots, its price, and the **Buy** button. Click on this button, enter your credit card or PayPal details, and complete the purchase as you would do with any other online store or service. After that Unity will offer to import the package. Click on the **Import** button and when Playmaker is downloaded, in the import window, leaving all the boxes checked, click on **Import** again. This will add the Playmaker files to your new Unity project.

Another way of installing Playmaker (or any other plugin for that matter) is going to **Assets | Import Package | Custom Package...**, provided that you already have the `unitypackage` file with it on your hard drive.

Playmaker also automatically imports some other popular Unity plugins it depends on: iTween for movement and animation and Photon for networking and multiplayer. We will talk about Photon later in *Chapter 6, Networking and Multiplayer*.

Chapter 1

Setting up your project

There is an important thing that you have to know about Unity: you can customize it in many different ways and even expand its interface with your own custom windows and panels. We are not going to discuss this just yet, as the user interface is examined in more detail in *Chapter 2, Unity's and Playmaker's User Interface*, but you should know that there is nothing to be surprised about if the user interface changes when you install a new extension, such as Playmaker. You can also drag different tabs around and see which layout fits your screen size/configuration and project best. Now we are going to set up the interface in a way that will simplify the explanations in the next couple of chapters. Once you are comfortable with the interface, you can feel free to customize it however you want.

If you haven't dragged anything around, you should be seeing the default Unity layout. If you have, go to **Window | Layouts** in the main menu and click on **Default** in order to reset to the default window layout. You will see a tab called **Hierarchy** on the left, **Scene** and **Game** in the middle, **Inspector** on the right, and **Project** and **Console** on the bottom. We will talk more about these tabs and their functions in *Chapter 2, Unity's and Playmaker's User Interface*. Right now, in order to save screen space, we will drag some of them around and change their appearance.

Getting Started with Unity and Playmaker

The following screenshot shows the default interface layout in Unity.

Let us start with the Project tab that you can see on the bottom of the screen. If it is not highlighted, click on the word **Project**. Right now both **Project** and **Console** tabs are pinned to the bottom of the screen, so you can switch between them in order to select one or the other. Unfortunately, this layout is not ideal, as in most cases you will need direct access to both **Project** and **Console** tabs at the same time. Click and drag the **Project** tab to the right of the **Scene** and **Game** tabs, until it snaps into place next to the **Inspector** tab. It will become tall and narrow.

Unfortunately, now there's very little space in the Project panel with those large icons. Luckily, Unity allows us to solve this problem easily by clicking on the small options icon () in the top-right corner of the **Project** panel and selecting **One Column Layout** from the list.

Now your **Project** panel will need much less space, and you will be able to see all of your project's file structure without getting frustrated over icons and sub-panels getting in your way.

> It is important to note here that some developers do prefer the **Two Column Layout** for its **Favorites** section and file manager-like subfolder representation; however, you will most likely want to have as much free work space as you can get, especially when working with plugins like Playmaker that add additional tabs that you need to have constant access to. You should consider the **Two Column Layout** only if you have a relatively big screen.

Now that the **Project** panel is set up and in place, let us free some more space for the **Hierarchy** panel by moving the **Console** panel under **Scene** and **Game**. To do this, click and drag the **Console** tab as you did with the **Project** tab, and move it to the bottom of the **Scene** and **Game** panels until it snaps into place directly under them.

The following screenshot shows what your editor window should look like if you followed all of the instructions in this chapter correctly.

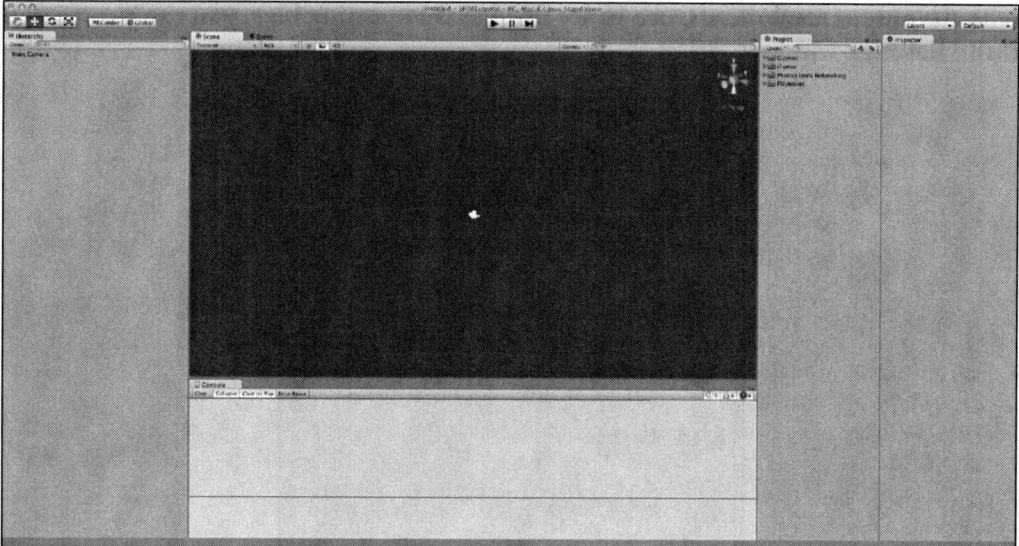

Finally, your work space is all set! Now it is time to change the project settings. It is a good idea to do this before you start working in order to get this out of the way, so let us get to it. We will not go into much detail about why certain project settings are set in a certain way, and most of them are quite self-explanatory.

First, select **Edit | Project Settings | Player** from the main menu. A new menu should appear in the **Inspector** panel on the right. You can put your name or the name of your company in the **Company Name** field near the top of the menu, and **Product Name** (just below it) by default should be the same as the name of your project folder that you specified while creating the project. Changing the project name will not rename your project folder. In fact, everything you change in the Player settings only affects the output game or application. We are going to be building a Unity WebPlayer project for this book's examples, so click on the tab with a little planet icon (⊕).

There are only two things here that we are interested in right now: screen resolution and WebPlayer template. Make sure that the **Default Screen Width** and **Height** are set to 960 and 600, respectively, and the active template is **No Context Menu**. There are more options here, but we are going to leave them at their default values for now.

Next, we will change the build settings to match our target platform. Go to **File | Build Settings...** and select **WebPlayer** from the list of available platforms (it should be the topmost item on the list). Then click on the **Switch Platform** button (as shown in the following screenshot). This will allow you to test the game directly with the output resolution. Once Unity finishes reimporting files, you can close the **Build Settings** window.

Summary

In this chapter you learned how to download and install Unity, purchase and install plugins for it from the Asset Store, prepare your project for work, optimize your workspace, and select the output platform. In the next chapter, we will look at Unity's interface in more detail. In particular, we will examine various panels and views (for example, **Inspector**, **Hierarchy**, **Game**, **Scene**) that you have encountered in this chapter and start using them.

2
Unity's and Playmaker's User Interface

In the previous chapter, we looked at the process of downloading and installing Unity, Playmaker, and setting up the project for work with this book. You have learned how to move the panels around within the Unity window in order to organize your workflow and how to change some of the project settings.

In this chapter, we will take a closer look at each Unity panel and interface element you have encountered so far, as well as some of those you have not seen, including the Playmaker's **Actions** panel and the **Finite State Machine** (**FSM**) view. You will also learn how to create simple game objects and modify their properties, such as position, location, and scale.

Interface overview and main menu

Unity's interface is modular: this means that you can drag its elements around, attach them to different parts of the Editor window or even detach them completely and put them on another screen for convenience. Editor is everything you see when you open Unity: panels, views, controls, and so on. *Editor* is how Unity itself is called within Unity. Let us take a look at the main interface elements.

Unity's and Playmaker's User Interface

There is the main menu on the top of the screen. Yours should include **File**, **Edit**, **Assets**, **GameObject**, **Component**, **PlayMaker**, **Window**, and **Help** submenus. They will help you create game objects (for example, primitives, lights, and cameras), attach components, and open new panels and views. The submenus can be explained as follows:

Submenus	Description
File	This submenu contains all the commands about building, saving, and opening projects and scenes. There are three commands here that you will use quite often, so it is a good idea to remember hotkeys for them: *command + S* (*Ctrl + S* in Windows) to save the current scene, *command + N* (*Ctrl + N* in Windows) to create a new scene, and *command + Shift + B* (*Ctrl + Shift + B* in Windows) to open the **Build Settings** window.
Edit	This submenu lets you perform various operations on files and game objects, such as copying (*command + C* or *Ctrl + C* in Windows), pasting (*command + V* or *Ctrl + V* in Windows), duplicating (*command + D* or *Ctrl + D* in Windows), and deleting (*command +Delete* or just *Delete* in Windows). There are also undo (*command + Z* or *Ctrl + Z* in Windows) and redo (*command + Shift + Z* or *Ctrl + Shift + Z* in Windows) commands under it. These are all standard commands that are the same across your operating system, so you should just assume that they work the same as they do in Finder (Windows Explorer) or TextEdit (Windows Notepad).
Assets	This submenu lets you create, import, and export files, also known as assets using the game development term. These can be scripts, animations, shaders, materials, and so on. The list of assets that are currently in your project can be seen in the **Project** panel. You will use commands available through this submenu later on in this chapter.
GameObject	This submenu lets you create new game objects. Not unlike the way the **Assets** submenu is linked to the **Project** panel, the **GameObject** submenu is linked to the **Hierarchy** panel. You will learn more about different types of game objects later when we talk about the panels and views in Unity. For now just remember that you can create a new empty game object by pressing *command + Shift + N* (*Ctrl + Shift + N* in Windows). This is something you will be doing a lot while working in Unity.
Component	This submenu lets you add new components to your game objects. This is very important, because an empty game object does not do anything, and it is invisible. By adding components to it, you can change its appearance and behavior. We will talk about components in more detail in the next chapter.

Submenus	Description
PlayMaker	This submenu is not a default Unity submenu; it was added to the main menu by the Playmaker plugin that you imported from the Asset Store. This Playmaker-dedicated submenu lets you access Playmaker components and panels, such as the FSM view and its panel that allow you to choose new actions and transitions for your objects. We will look at Playmaker later on in this and the following chapters.
Window	This submenu lets you open new panels and views, such as **Asset Store**, **Hierarchy**, and **Scene**. This submenu is useful if you have lost or accidentally closed one of your panels or views and want to find or open it again. It doesn't allow you to open multiple instances of the same interface elements, so you will always find the existing panel if it is open already.
Help	This submenu allows you to access useful Unity reference resources, such as Unity Manual, Reference Material, and Scripting Reference. There are copies of these available on the web, but it is always a good idea to use the ones provided with your installation: this way you are making sure that the documentation you are using is consistent with your version of Unity, plus the local copy of the documentation always works faster. The **Help** submenu also provides shortcuts to Unity's community sites, such as forum, answers, and feedback, and lets you report bugs and check for updates.

Now, below the main menu is the toolbar that includes (left to right) main controls for the **Scene** view, game execution controls, and drop-down boxes of layer filter and layout selection.

Under the toolbar you will see the panel and the view tabs. We will look at them closer later in this chapter, but for now you just need to know that there is a distinction between views that include **Scene** and **Game** and panels that include **Hierarchy**, **Console**, **Project**, and **Inspector**. Panels and views can all be manipulated, resized, detached, and attached in the same way, but the difference between them is that views (as the name suggests) let you see your game scene in one way or another, while panels provide additional information and tools for game objects, the scene, or the project as a whole.

Unity's and Playmaker's User Interface

> Keep in mind that the distinction between views and panels is merely a helpful convention and by no means limits the functionality of a tab. This is especially true of custom tabs added by various plugins or, indeed, by yourself. In this book this distinction is made for convenience.

The following figure shows what your Editor window is supposed to look like if you haven't moved any tabs around since *Chapter 1, Getting Started with Unity and Playmaker*. We will be referring to this layout throughout this chapter, so if your layout differs, I suggest you change it to match the image. You can always go back to it later.

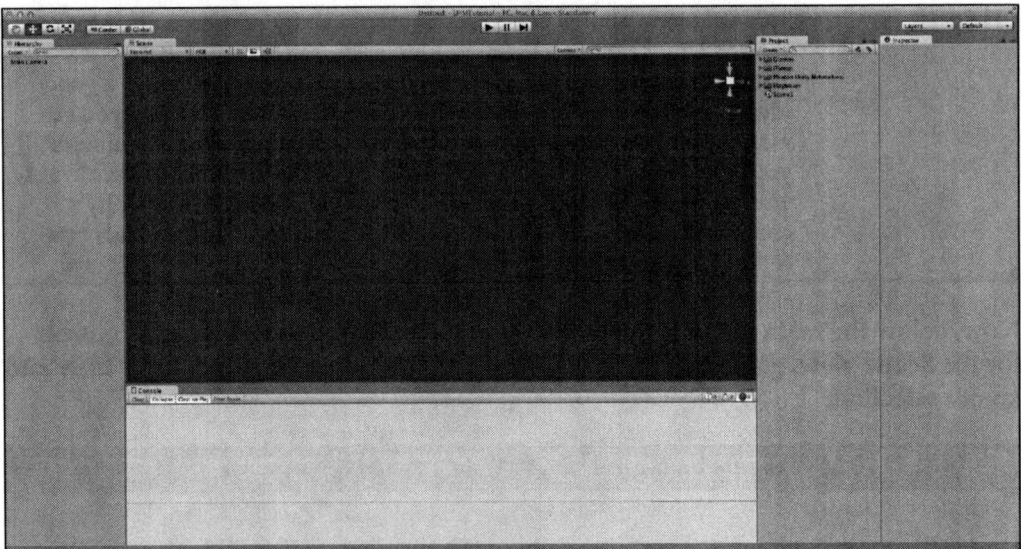

On the very bottom of the Unity Editor window there is a long empty gray line. This is the status bar: it shows the last thing displayed in the **Console** panel, and clicking on it reveals the **Console**, highlighting the last log message in it. The status bar, the main menu, and the toolbar are all permanent interface elements in Unity and, unlike the tabs, cannot be closed, detached, or resized without manipulating the Editor window itself.

Hierarchy panel

A panel in Unity is a tab that provides information about or gives you additional control over a game object, a scene, or the project as a whole. Panels can be added, closed, detached, and attached at will. You can drag them around as you see fit in order to optimize your workflow. If you followed the instructions in *Chapter 1, Getting Started with Unity and Playmaker*, your current layout should match that of the last screenshot in the previous section of this chapter.

To begin, let us look at the Hierarchy panel (you should have it attached on the left of the Editor window).

The place where you see the word **Hierarchy** written is the tab's header. You can drag any tab by its header, be it a view or a panel. Any number of panels can be present in any position in the Editor, so sometimes you will have a situation when you have multiple tabs attached to the same area of the screen (as on the following figure):

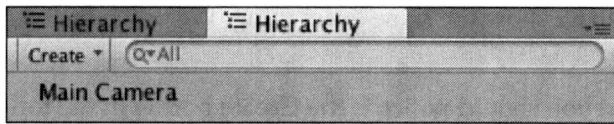

Let us try to reproduce this situation. Click the **Options** (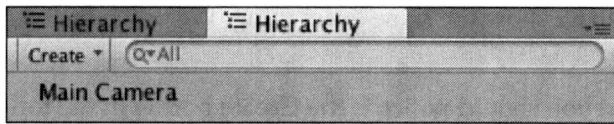) button in the top-right corner of the Hierarchy panel. Then hover the **Add Tab** option from the drop-down list and, finally, click on **Hierarchy**. Now you should have two **Hierarchy** panels attached to the same side of the screen. Their headers should be next to each other: one of them active, and the other one inactive. The active panel is the one that has a lighter color.

The following figure shows the menu that allows you to add new tabs to a certain area of the screen; in this case it is on the right, in the same place where the **Hierarchy** panel is. Use it to add another **Hierarchy** panel.

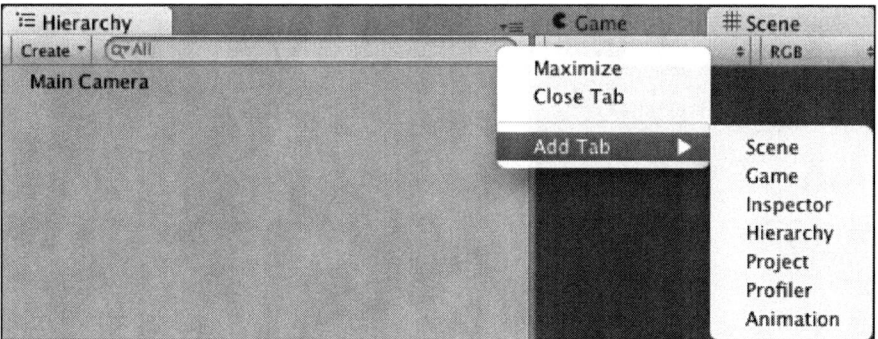

[23]

Click on the inactive panel's header to see its contents. At this point you should see that both panels look exactly the same: the only thing inside both is **Main Camera**. This is because both panels show the contents of the same scene. You can have as many **Hierarchy** panels as you want, but they will all show exactly the same thing. We don't need two of them, so let us close one: right click on one of the Hierarchy tabs' headers and choose **Close Tab** from the contextual menu that appears. Note that this is the same menu that appears when you click on the **Options** button in the top-right corner of the panel. This is just another way of doing the same thing.

I have just mentioned something called scene and a scene's contents—but what does it mean? A project in Unity is composed of scenes; think of them as level files if you like, except apart from the actual game levels, scenes can contain things like intro cinematics, loading screens, game menus, or anything. This is just a convenient way of dividing your game into manageable chunks, and the **Hierarchy** panel reveals everything that is inside of the currently open scene. You can have only one scene open at any given moment, which is why no matter how many **Hierarchy** panels you open, they will all show the same exact thing. We will talk about scenes in more detail in the next chapter.

Another thing that you should notice is the **Create** button in the top-left corner of the panel just below the header. Click on it, and you will see the same menu that you would see if you navigated to **GameObject | Other** from the main menu. This menu allows you to create game objects that are added to the current scene when you click on their names in the list.

A game object in Unity is kind of a shell, a container that can be anything: a cube, a light, a camera, or a character. Go ahead and create a cube, a quad, and a directional light. We will use these in the following chapters to create a game.

Now that we have all these game objects, we want to position them in a certain way in the scene. To do this, we are going to use the Inspector panel, among other things.

Inspector panel

The main purpose of the **Inspector** panel is performing various actions on game objects, including changing their properties, such as appearance, behavior, position, size, and rotation. Select the **Cube** game object in the **Hierarchy** panel by clicking on it once. The appearance of the **Inspector** panel should now change to include a number of things displayed in the following screenshot:

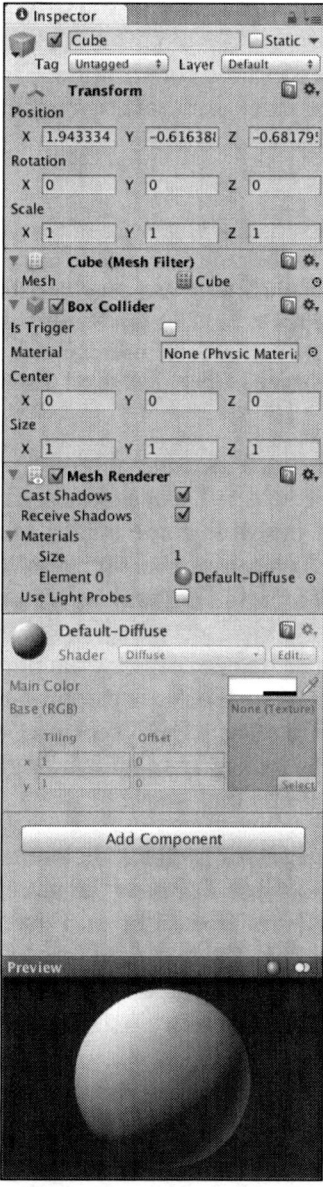

Unity's and Playmaker's User Interface

The first thing that you should notice is the small padlock (🔒) icon in the top-right corner of the panel next to the **Options** button. Unlike the **Hierarchy** panel, **Inspector** shows properties of an object rather than a scene, and, since you can have any number of game objects in your currently active scene at the same time, you can assign different inspectors to always focus on specific objects. Open a new **Inspector** tab by right-clicking the **Inspector** header and selecting **Add Tab | Inspector**. Both inspectors will be focused on the cube that you selected in **Hierarchy**. Click on the padlock icon in one of the inspectors. This will make this **Inspector** always display the properties of **Cube**, so, if you select **Quad** in **Hierarchy**, the locked (🔒) Inspector will continue showing the Cube's properties, while the other one will show **Quad**. You can verify this by clicking on the headers of the two **Inspector** panels that you have opened.

> If you want to expose the properties of two objects at the same time without having to click on the headers, you can detach one of the **Inspector** panels by clicking and dragging its header wherever you want that panel to be. This can be helpful if you want to copy components or properties from one object to another or if you want to keep one important object always on display.

Make sure you are comfortable with the idea of having multiple inspectors and the fact that they correspond to the selected game object. Also note that an **Inspector** panel can expose properties of multiple game objects at the same time. You can select multiple game objects in the **Hierarchy** panel by pressing and holding *command* (*Ctrl* in Windows). You can also press *Shift* and select a range of game objects. These operations are similar to those you would perform in Finder (or Windows Explorer). Try doing this a few times until you are comfortable performing these actions in the **Hierarchy** panel and always take note of how the contents of the unlocked **Inspector** panel change based on the game objects that you select. Once you feel like you have experimented enough, close the locked **Inspector** by right-clicking its header and selecting **Close Tab** from the contextual menu.

Just below the header in the **Inspector** panel is the name of the selected game object. You can change it however you want. For now, let us rename our **Cube** Wall. Make sure that you have **Cube** selected in **Hierarchy** and that its properties are displayed in the **Inspector** panel. Click within the text field where you see **Cube** written at the moment, delete everything, and type Wall, then press *return* (*Enter*). You will notice that the name has changed in the **Hierarchy** panel as well.

Below the name field there is a long section with various components separated by black horizontal lines. A default cube (now called **Wall**) has **Transform**, **Mesh Filter**, **Box Collider,** and **Mesh Renderer** components. We will closely examine the components in the next chapter. For now you should focus on the Transform component (shown in the following image along with the **Inspector** panel header), which is the only component that every game object in Unity has.

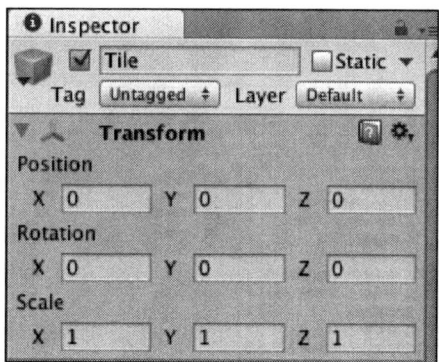

Transform defines position, rotation, and scale of a game object in 3D space. These are all its properties. Set the position of **Wall** to (0, 0.5, 0) by clicking in the **X**, **Y**, and **Z** fields, deleting everything in there, entering the value you want instead, and pressing *return* (*Enter*) on your keyboard. You have just changed the position property of the **Transform** component of the **Wall** game object. The next chapter will examine properties and components more closely. For now just set the positions and rotations of the game objects you have in the scene to the following values:

Name	Position	Rotation
Directional light	0, 0, 0	50, -30, 0
Main Camera	0, 10, 0	90, 0, 0
Quad	0, 0, 0	90, 0, 0
Wall	0, 0.5, 0	0, 0, 0

For now, we will leave the **Scale** property of all the objects at its default value (1, 1, 1).

Now that you have modified your scene, you might want to save it. Press *command + S* (*Ctrl + S* in Windows). A dialog window should appear asking you where you would like to save your scene. By default it should offer to save it in the `Assets` folder. Name your scene `Scene1` and click on **Save**. The following screenshot shows the path where the scene file should be saved. Note that you cannot save the scene outside of the `Assets` folder. If you try, an error message will pop-up warning you about it.

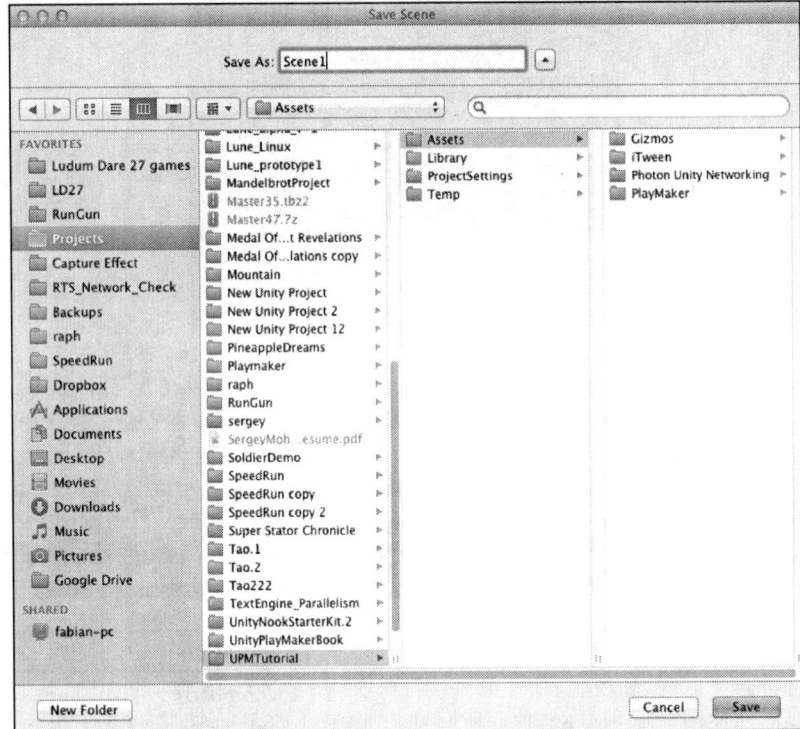

Project panel

Have a look at the **Project** panel: you should have four folders and a file called `Scene1` displayed there. The **Project** panel is your project's file browser, similar to Mac OSX Finder or Windows Explorer, but it only shows files and folders that are situated inside the `Assets` folder of your project.

Unlike **Hierarchy** and **Inspector**, **Project** (see the following screenshot) always displays the same thing as long as you have the same Unity project open. All of the scene files, scripts, and art assets are shown and can be manipulated from here. Using the icons to the right of the search field, you can filter the things displayed in the **Project** panel either by tag or by type.

Chapter 2

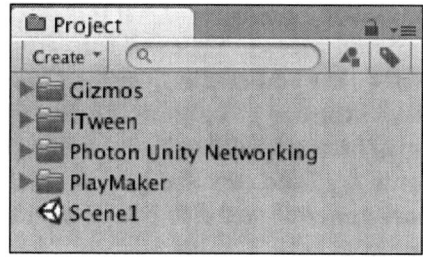

It is generally a good practice to keep your project's file structure well-organized, as it helps to increase productivity and save time looking for files. To organize your assets, you can put things inside folders with clear names, such as Artwork, Scripts, or Music. To begin with, let us try to organize what we have in our **Project** panel already.

Click on the **Create** button in the top-left corner of the panel; this should reveal a menu that allows you to create different types of assets. This is the same menu you get by going to **Assets** | **Create** in the main menu.

 The third way to access the **Assets** menu is right-clicking anywhere in the empty area below the list of files in the **Project** panel and clicking on **Create** in the contextual menu that appears.

Create a folder called Scenes. In order to rename a folder if you forgot to enter a name when the folder was just created, press *return* (or *F2* if you are using Windows). Once you have it named appropriately, click and drag the Scene1 file and drop it into the Scenes folder. From now on, we will save all of the scenes into that folder instead of the Assets root. This way, they will be easier to find when we want to open a specific scene.

Views

Now that the Project panel is well-organized and your objects are positioned in the scene, it is time to have a look at the view tabs: **Game** and **Scene**. The former shows the output of all the cameras, while the latter is your main workspace in Unity. This is where the level design is done. The **Game** view becomes interactive when you click on the play button in the toolbar (▶) or use the hotkey *command* + *P* (or *Ctrl* + *P* in Windows), provided there is some kind of input defined in Playmaker or other components. You can also pause (∥) the game by pressing *command* + *Shift* + *P* (*Ctrl* + *Shift* + *P* in Windows). This is how you will test your game later. Right now there are no interactions yet, but we will get to that soon enough.

Unity's and Playmaker's User Interface

Activate the **Scene** view by clicking on its header if it is not active right now. In the **Hierarchy** panel, select **Wall** and press *F*. This will focus the **Scene** view on **Wall**. You should be seeing the cube that you created, with a **Quad** and **Directional light** gizmo below it (it looks like a little sun). A **gizmo** is generally a 2D element in 3D space that lets you select and/or manipulate objects even if they are not represented in any other way in the scene. A gizmo can also be non-interactive, such as a simple line or a wire cube. These are generally used to reveal position or direction of something otherwise invisible.

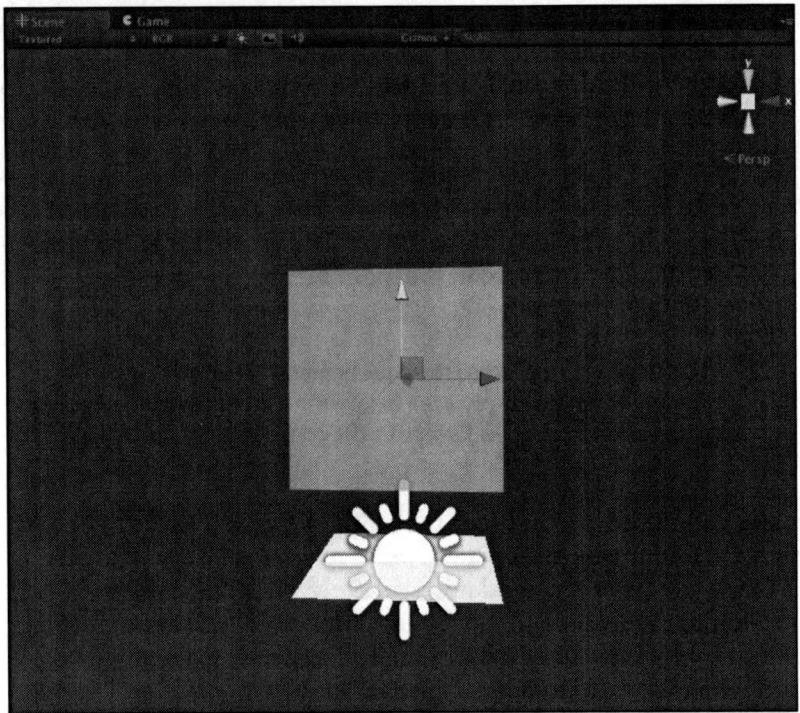

Selecting an object and pressing *F* is one way to navigate the 3D space. Another way is using your mouse. You can select different objects directly in the **Scene** view by clicking on their meshes (3D models) or gizmos. To look around, press and hold the right mouse button while moving your mouse in the **Scene** view. Zoom in and out by using your scroll wheel. Use middle click to drag the view around. You can also rotate around a point by pressing and holding *Alt* and clicking the left mouse button and moving your mouse around.

Click on the **Directional light** gizmo and press *W* or [icon] in the toolbar. You should see three arrows appear: red, green, and blue. These arrows correspond to the X, Y, and Z axes in 3D space, respectively. Clicking and dragging one of the arrows will move the object in space. Move **Directional light** anywhere you want: its position does not matter. What does matter, however, is its rotation.

Press *E* or [icon] in the toolbar. A sphere with colored and white circles will appear around the object. Each colored circle is responsible for the object's rotation around one axis. Once again: red for X, green for Y and blue for Z. When you select your light, you should also see yellow rays coming out of it. This is a gizmo that shows in what direction your **Directional light** is lighting the scene. Rotate **Directional light** in such a way that **Wall** and **Quad** appear well-lit, almost white in the **Game** view. Do not forget that you can switch between the **Game** and **Scene** views at any moment to see a preview of what you will see in the game.

You can also switch between the ways your rotation, position, and scale gizmos appear by clicking the **Global/Local** toggle button in the toolbar. The **Pivot/Center** toggle button determines where it appears: in the pivot point of the object or in its geometric center.

Once you are happy with the light, select the **Quad** object and press *R* or [icon] in the toolbar. This is the scale manipulation mode. If you press *F* to focus on **Quad**, you will see a gizmo similar to that of the movement manipulator, but with little colored cubes instead of arrows on the ends of each line. As before, colors correspond to axes: red for X, green for Y, and blue for Z. There is also a white cube in the middle, which is the uniform scale manipulator that allows you to change scale on all three axes at the same time.

Using this gizmo, scale **Quad** to be about `100` on the X and Y axes. Its Z scale should stay the same. You can check the current values of position, rotation, and scale in the **Transform** component in the **Inspector** panel when you have an object selected.

Save your scene by pressing *command + S* (*Ctrl + S* in Windows).

Playmaker interface

It is time to finally take a look at Playmaker. In the main menu, go to **PlayMaker | PlayMaker Editor**. A welcome window with different Playmaker options and a **playMaker** panel should appear. Close the welcome window, then attach the **playMaker** panel to the same region of the Editor where you have your **Console** panel as shown in the following screenshot (this should be just below the **Scene** and **Game** views if you haven't changed anything since *Chapter 1, Getting Started with Unity and Playmaker*).

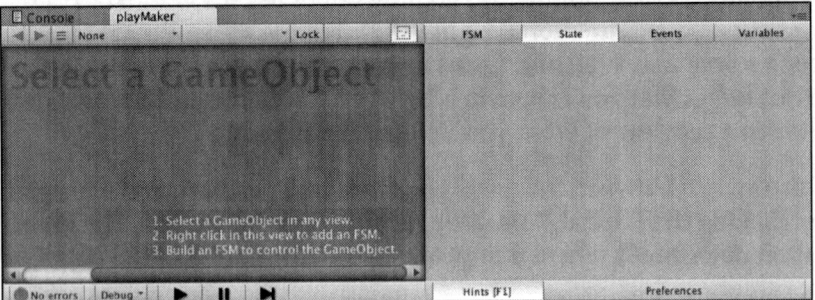

The darker area on the left is the FSM view.

> Keep in mind that the FSM view is called Playmaker Editor in the official Playmaker documentation. In this book we will use a clearer name, *FSM view*, to distinguish between different areas of the **playMaker** panel.

It is here that you will edit your finite state machines and create state nodes and transitions between them, which we will talk about in more detail in the next chapter. For now, follow the instructions given in the lower-right corner of the FSM view:

1. Select the **Wall** game object in the **Hierarchy** panel or in the **Scene** view by clicking on it.

2. Right-click anywhere in the FSM view and select **Add FSM** from the contextual menu that appears to add a finite state machine to the **Wall** game object. When you do that, note the red icon that appears next to **Wall** in the **Hierarchy** panel. This icon means that the object has a Playmaker FSM component. Also note the Playmaker FSM component that appeared in the **Inspector** panel.

3. Now you can manipulate FSM to assign various behaviors to **Wall**. Read all the tips displayed in the **playMaker** panel carefully.

Chapter 2

 To take a better look at any one of the tabs, including the **playMaker** panel, press the *Space* key with your mouse cursor hovering over the tab. Then press space again to minimize. You can do this with any view or panel in the Unity Editor.

On the right side of the **playMaker** panel, there are tabs that display and let you modify different information types, including the FSM as a whole, as well as its states, events, and variables. Click on each tab and examine the tips in grey rectangles explaining the contents of each tab. Once you are done with the tips, you can press the **Hint** toggle button on the bottom of the panel to disable them. You can also do this by pressing *F1*. Before you do that, click on the **Preferences** button next to it and read the tips there. We will examine the necessary changes to the Playmaker preferences in the next chapter.

Under the FSM view you should see controls similar to pause/play in the toolbar. These are, in fact, the same buttons, and are there just to make it more convenient for you to control the game when you are working with Playmaker.

The second most important Playmaker-related panel is the **Action Browser**. You can open it by selecting **PlayMaker | Editor Window | Action Browser** from the main menu. A part of the **Actions** panel is shown in the following screenshot:

Drag it by its header to the right side of the Editor until it snaps into the same area of the screen as **Inspector**. This panel shows categories of actions that you have in your Playmaker library. Clicking on one of the categories, for example, **Camera,** will reveal the actions. There is also a search bar near the top of the panel that allows you to access the actions you need faster. When you select an action, for example, **Camera | Screen To World Point**, a preview of its parameters appears on the bottom of the panel. It shows what the selected action will look like in the **State** tab of the **playMaker** panel. If you have a Playmaker-enabled object and a state in the FSM view selected, you can add an action to it by clicking the **Add Action To State** button in the bottom-right corner of the **Actions** panel.

You can press the play button (or use the shortcut *command + P* or *Ctrl + P* Windows) to see that there are no errors and everything is working properly. When you are done, press play again and save the scene.

Summary

In this chapter, you examined some of the main interface elements in Unity and Playmaker, added some objects to the scene and manipulated those objects. You also looked at game objects and components and learned about properties of components. These subjects will be examined in more detail in the next chapter. The scene that you created in this chapter lays a foundation for creating a game, and all objects that you have created and manipulated so far are going to be used in the final game.

3
Components and State Machines

In the previous chapter, we learned about Unity's interface, and the way things are organized and displayed in the Editor. You added a FSM to a game object and briefly looked at the interface elements related to Playmaker. You also manipulated game objects and components using such interface elements as the **Hierarchy** and **Inspector** panels, as well as the **Scene** view. In this chapter we will cover:

- The Component-based approach to game development that Unity relies on
- Game objects, components, and their properties in more detail
- The interchangeable nature of game objects when using components to define appearance and behavior
- Finite state machines, actions, and transitions
- Making simple game mechanics using Playmaker

Game objects, components, and properties

Unity works using a popular and common approach for game development, which is called the component-based architecture. This approach is widely used in software development to make things more reusable and easier to manage.

Let us talk about the way things are organized in Unity. Some of them have already been mentioned in previous chapters, but I will repeat them briefly so that you can see the game objects, components, and their properties in the larger context.

First of all, you have a project, which is essentially a folder that contains all of the files and information about your game. Some of the files are called scenes (think of them as levels). A scene contains a number of game objects that you have added to it. The contents of your scenes are determined by you, and you can have as many of them as you want. You can also make your game switch between different scenes, thus making different sets of game objects active.

On a smaller scale, you have game objects and components. A game object by itself is simply an invisible container that does not do anything. Without adding appropriate components to it, it cannot, for instance, appear in the scene, receive input from the player, or move and interact with other objects. Using components, you can easily assemble powerful game objects while reusing several small parts, each responsible for a simple task or behavior—rendering the game object, handling the input, taking damage, playing an audio effect, and so on—making your game much simpler to develop and manage. Unity relies heavily on this approach, so the better you grasp it, the faster you will get good at it.

The only component that each and every game object in Unity has attached to it by default is **Transform**. It lets you define the game object's position, rotation, and scale. Normally, you can attach, detach, and destroy components in any given game object at will, but you cannot remove **Transform**.

Each component has a number of properties that you can access and change: these can be integer or floating point numbers, strings of text, textures, scripts, references to game objects or other components. They are used to change the way a certain component behaves, to influence its appearance or interaction. Some of the properties that you have already encountered in *Chapter 2, Unity's and Playmaker's User Interface*, include the position, rotation, and scale properties of the **Transform** component. There are others that you have seen, including FSM, that we will talk about later in this chapter.

The following screenshot shows the **Wall** game object with the **Transform**, **Mesh Filter**, **Box Collider**, **Mesh Renderer**, and **Script** components attached to it. the properties of **Transform** are displayed. In order to reveal or hide a component's properties you need to left-click on its name or on the small arrow on the left of its icon.

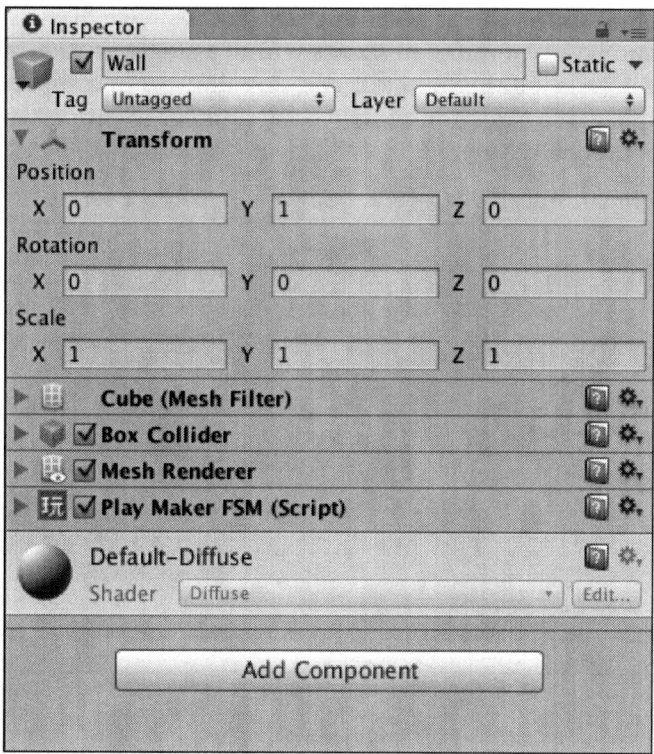

Unity has a number of predefined game objects that already have components attached to them, such as cameras, lights, and primitives. You can access them by choosing **GameObject | Create** from the main menu. Alternatively, you can create empty game objects by pressing *command + Shift + N* (*Ctrl + Shift + N* in Windows) and attach components to them using the **Components** submenu.

The following figure shows the project structure that we have discussed. Note that there can be any number of scenes within a single project, any number of game objects within a single scene, any number of components attached to a single game object, and finally, any number of properties within a single component.

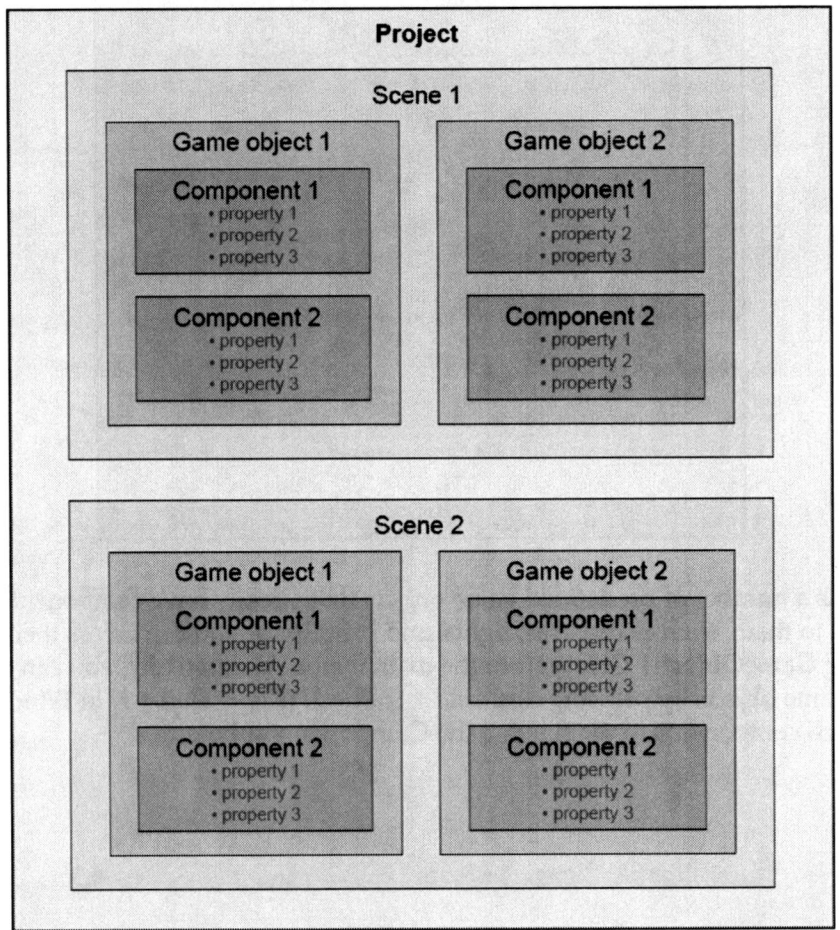

One final thing that you need to know about components right now is that you can copy them by right-clicking on the name of the component in the **Inspector** panel and selecting **Copy Component** from the contextual menu shown in the following screenshot. You can also reset the properties of the components to their default values, remove components, and move them up or down for your convenience.

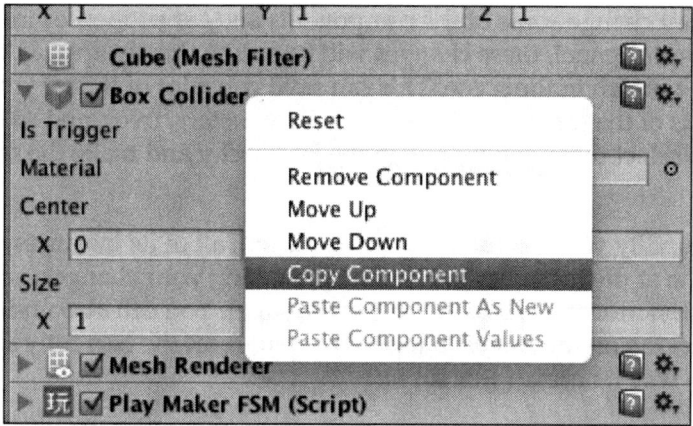

The copied component can be pasted by right-clicking any component's name in the **Inspector** panel and selecting either **Paste Component As New** or **Paste Component Values** from the same contextual menu. The difference between these two commands is that the former will add a new component identical to the one that you have copied, while the latter will simply transfer the values of all the properties. These commands become active once you have copied a component.

Working with prefabs

In order to create multiple instances of a game object with the same components and properties, or access the same game object from different scenes, you can save it as a file in your Assets folder. These files are called prefabs in Unity and act like game object templates. To create an empty prefab, right-click on the empty space in the **Project** panel, then select **Create | Prefab** from the contextual menu. A new file called New Prefab should appear in the **Project** panel. Call this prefab Wall. Now create an empty folder called Prefabs and put the Wall prefab in this folder.

Right now the prefab is empty.

1. In the **Hierarchy** panel, select the **Wall** game object that you created in *Chapter 2, Unity's and Playmaker's User Interface*. Click and drag it into the Wall prefab in the **Project** panel.
2. The name of the **Wall** game object will become blue in **Hierarchy**, and when you select the Wall prefab, you will see all of the components that the original **Wall** game object had in the **Inspector** panel.

Now, if you drag-and-drop the Wall prefab into the scene, a new object called **Wall** will be created with exactly the same properties as those defined in the prefab.

Moreover, if you change some of the components and/or properties in the prefab using the **Inspector** panel, these changes will be automatically applied to all the instances of the prefab in the scene. This can save you a lot of time if you have multiple objects of the same type (that is, walls, monsters, trees, and so on) as you do not have to select them one-by-one in the **Hierarchy** and make the same changes multiple times.

You can also modify your prefab (and, by extension, all of its instances in the scene) by selecting one of the instances in **Hierarchy**, making your changes, and clicking the **Apply** button near the top of the **Inspector** panel. You can also undo all of the changes by clicking on the **Revert** button. This will reset the currently selected instance to the way its prefab was set up.

This works because, in fact, all the components and properties of an instance are linked to the ones of the prefab. Only when you change them in the instance they become unlinked, which means that further updates of that property on the prefab won't be applied to this instance. These unlinked properties can be distinguished because their name becomes bold in the **Inspector** panel. If you want to re-link a specific unlinked property you can right-click on it and select **Revert value to Prefab**.

Besides the **Apply** and **Revert** buttons, all prefab instances also have a **Select** button. This button lets you select and highlight the prefab corresponding to the currently selected instance in the **Project** panel, so you can access it more easily. Moreover, as we saw earlier, a prefab instance can be easily identified by its blue tinted name in the **Hierarchy** panel. The alternative way of creating a prefab is even simpler: you can simply drag-and-drop a game object from the **Hierarchy** panel into the **Project** panel. An appropriately named file will be created in the `Assets` folder.

Another very important thing to know about prefabs is that they can be copied and shared on the Web, since they are little more than the files recognized by Unity that contain information about components and properties. Now, follow these steps to modify the `Wall` prefab to suit our needs better:

1. Create a new folder in the **Project** panel and call it `Materials`. It will contain material files that contain information about textures, shaders, and colors of your game objects.
2. Create a new material file by clicking on the **Create** button in the top-left corner of the **Project** panel and selecting **Material** from the drop-down list.
3. Name the new material `WallMaterial` and put it inside the `Materials` folder.

4. Select **WallMaterial** in the **Project** panel, then in **Inspector**, click on the rectangle next to the text that says **Main Color**. In the **Color** window that appears, select the black color and close the **Color** window. The following screenshot shows the **Material** modification interface as well as the **Color** window:

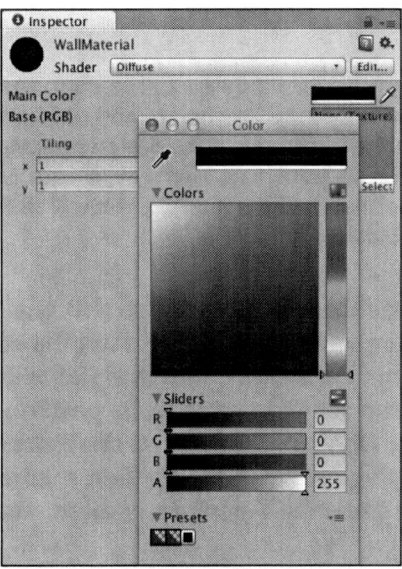

5. Now that you have this new material set up, select the `Wall` prefab, then drag-and-drop **WallMaterial** into the **Element 0** element of the **Materials** property of the prefab's **Mesh Renderer** component. It should replace **Default Diffuse**. The following screenshot shows what the **Mesh Renderer** component should look like once your are done assigning the new material.

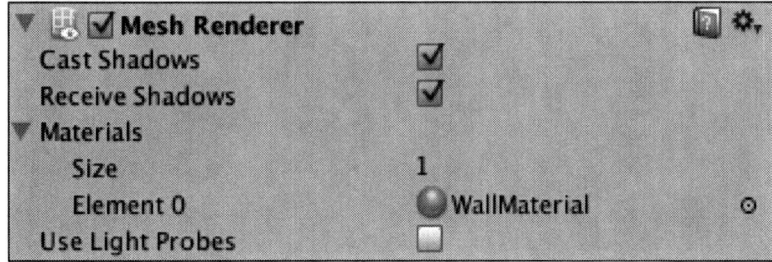

6. Now all of the instances of the `Wall` prefab will be black.
7. Also, set the X scale property of the **Transform** component to `15`. This will make all the new walls longer.

8. Select the **Main Camera** game object and set its **Projection** property of the **Camera** component to **Orthographic** using the **Inspector** panel. This will make the view of the camera flat; the game view will now appear two-dimensional.

9. Set the **Size** property to 5. You can adjust the look later, but for now this will help us focus on gameplay.

> It is often a good idea to restrict yourself to simple primitives, color-coded untextured materials, and orthographic projection cameras in the beginning of the design process, because it will let you focus on gameplay. This way, if your game is fun, you will know about it, and if it is not, you will not get distracted by fancy visuals.

Make four walls and arrange them in the scene so that what you see in the **Game** view looks like the following screenshot. If this is not the case, you can go back to the table in *Chapter 2, Unity's and Playmaker's User Interface*, and see if your **Main Camera** game object is positioned and rotated correctly. Its position should be set to (0, 10, 0) and rotation to (90, 0, 0). Don't forget that you can rotate the objects to precise values such as 90 and 180 degrees by changing their rotation angle in the **Transform** component. Also make sure that the Y position of all the walls remains equal to 0.5.

Chapter 3

Finite state machines, states, and actions

We have talked about game objects and components. Now it is time to have a look at Playmaker FSMs, states, and actions in them.

An FSM in Playmaker is a graph that consists of states and transitions between them, attached to a game object. It allows for a way of visual programming using different states of the graph and events that trigger transitions to other states.

If you select the `Wall` prefab and open the **playMaker** panel, you will see that its FSM has two states: the default **Start** state where everything begins and another one called **State 1** by default, with an arrow connecting the former to the latter. The arrow is a transition. You cannot remove the Start state or the one it is connected to, because if you could you would not need the FSM attached to the object. However, you can create new states and define transitions to them.

> You can navigate the FSM view almost exactly the same way you would do the **Scene** view. Use the middle mouse button to drag the view. Use the left mouse button to move the states around. This does not change anything in the logic of the state machine, but lets you organize everything the way that makes sense to you, as well as look at the parts of the graph that you are most interested in at the moment if the whole state machine is too big to be shown at once.

A state in FSM is empty by default and does not do anything, a lot like an empty game object without any components attached to it. In order to make a state do something, you need to attach actions to it.

As we have seen in *Chapter 2, Unity's and Playmaker's User Interface*, you can add an FSM to an object by selecting the latter, right-clicking in the FSM view of the **playMaker** panel, and then selecting **Add FSM** from the contextual menu. You can remove an object from the Playmaker control by right-clicking the header of the Playmaker FSM (**Script**) component in **Inspector** and selecting **Remove Component** from the contextual menu. This will remove the FSM and erase all of the changes you made to it, including added states and transitions. An object has an FSM attached to it if there is a red Playmaker hieroglyph icon () next to its name in the **Hierarchy** panel.

As an example for this book, we will be making a version of the classic air hockey game. In order to begin, we will need to add a puck and a mallet. In this chapter, you will make the mallet move based on the mouse position and push the puck as you would expect it to do in real life.

Components and State Machines

Right now in your scene there are four walls, a background quad, a camera, and a directional light (created in *Chapter 2, Unity's and Playmaker's User Interface*). Now it is time to make things interactive. Let us start with a mallet.

1. Create a new cylinder primitive by selecting **GameObject | Create Other | Cylinder** in the main menu.

2. Rename this game object to Mallet and make a dark green (RGB color set to 10, 155, 10 in the **Color** window) material called **MalletMaterial** for it, then assign the material to it, as you did for the Wall prefab before.

3. Set the scale of **Mallet** to (1.35, 1.35, 1.35) and its position to (-6.5, 1.45, 0).

4. Now we are going to make the mallet move. First of all, we need to add a component called **Character Controller** to it. This component is in charge of character physics. Select **Mallet**, then click on the **Add Component** button near the bottom of the **Inspector** panel. Type Character Controller in the search bar, and then double-click on the **Character Controller** item in the list (as shown in the following screenshot). When Unity asks you if you want to replace the existing **CapsuleCollider** component, click on **Replace**.

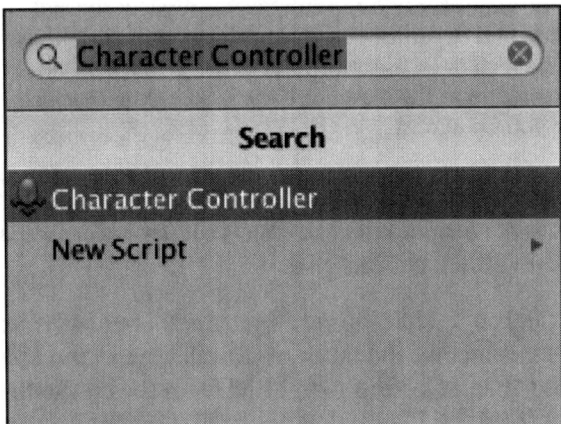

5. In the **Character Controller** component, set the **Skin Width** property to 0 (it will be set to the minimum possible value, which is 0.0001). We are doing this to make sure that our mallet's collisions look precise.

6. Add an FSM to Mallet by selecting it, right-clicking in the FSM view of the **playMaker** panel, and selecting **Add FSM** from the contextual menu.

7. Select **State 1**, then in the **State** tab on the right of the **playMaker** panel enter Move in the first text field from the top. It is responsible for the name of the currently selected state. When you enter the new name, you should see the state change in the FSM view as well.

[44]

8. Keeping the **Move** state selected, open the **Actions** panel (it should be attached to the same area of the **Editor** window as the **Inspector** panel; alternatively, click on the **Action Browser** button on the bottom-right of the **State** tab) and find the **Mouse Pick** action under the **Input** category. Click on it, then click on the **Add Action To State** button in the bottom-right corner of the panel. You should notice that the **Mouse Pick** action appeared in the **State** tab of the **playMaker** panel.

   This action gets the cursor position in 3D space when you hover an object. Under the hood it draws an invisible ray (this action is called **raycast**) from the mouse position on the camera's near clipping plane (you can see it as one of the white gizmo rectangles in the **Scene** view when you select **Main Camera**). If there is something in the way of the ray, a ray hit gets detected, and Unity finds out where exactly it happened. In our case, we will use the background quad to get the position of the mouse cursor, and then make the mallet follow it.

9. In order to pick a correct ray-hit position, we need to make sure that nothing else gets in the way of the ray. To do this, we will tell the ray to interact only with the background quad. Select the **Quad** game object and rename it Background for clarity. Then find the **Layer** drop-down menu in the top-right corner of the **Inspector** panel, click on the drop-down button that says **Default** by default, and press **Add Layer...** in it. The appearance of **Inspector** should now change to reveal a list of tags and layers as shown in the following screenshot:

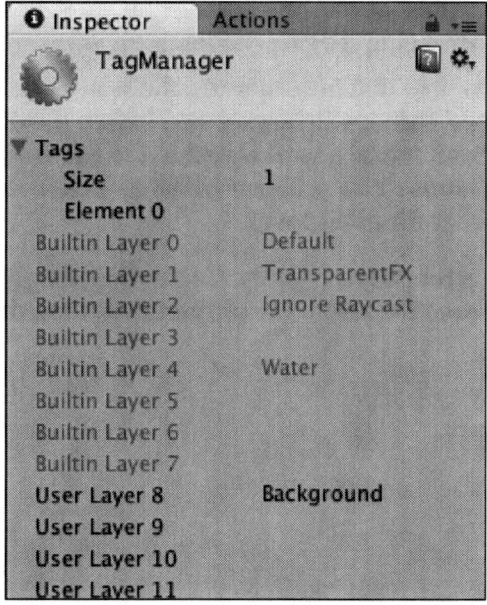

Components and State Machines

This menu is called **TagManager**. Click on the right of **User Layer 8** and enter Background in the edit field that appears, then press *Return* on your keyboard. Select the **Background** object again and set its layer to **Background** by choosing the appropriate element from the drop-down **Layer** list you used to access the **TagManager** before.

10. Select **Mallet** again. In the **Mouse Pick** action of the **Move** state, set the **Layer Mask** parameter to 1. This determines how many layers you will set to interact with the raycast. **Element 0** should appear below. In the drop-down list to its right, select the **Background** layer you created before.

11. From now on, the raycast in the **Mouse Pick** action will ignore all objects that are not in the **Background** layer. Now we need to store the ray-hit position in a variable. Go to the **Variable** tab of the **playMaker** panel and enter mousePos in the **New Variable** field on the bottom. Click on the **Add** button. Set the **Variable Type** to **Vector3**. A **Vector 3** variable contains three numbers: **X**, **Y**, and **Z**.

12. Go back to the **State** tab and set the **Store Point** property of the **Mouse Pick** action to **mousePos**. This will save the position of the ray hit in the **Vector3** type variable that you just created. Finally, check the **Every Frame** property checkbox on the bottom of the **Mouse Pick** action to make sure that the mouse position is updated continuously as opposed to just once in the beginning of the game.

13. Add the action called **Controller Simple Move** located under the **Character** category of the **Actions** panel to your **Move** state. It should appear just below the **Mouse Pick** action. If it appears above it, you can move it down by clicking and dragging it by its header.

    It is important to note that the order of actions in the state matters: the actions mentioned earlier will be executed before the ones that are mentioned later, so if you want to use a variable set in the **Mouse Pick** action, you must make sure that **Mouse Pick** is above whatever action is going to use it (in our case it is **Controller Simple Move**).

14. Set the **Move Vector** property of the **Controller Simple Move** action to **mousePos**. Leave the rest of the properties at their default values.

Interaction between game objects

Now that the mallet moves, we are going to make it interact with a puck. When the mallet touches the puck, we are going to apply a force to it in the opposite direction.

You can click the Play button in the toolbar and see how the mallet moves based on the mouse position. You will notice that it collides with the walls, follows the mouse cursor smoothly, and changes its movement speed based on how fast and far you move your mouse.

1. Create another cylinder called **Puck** and place it in (`-3, 0.85, 0`). Set its scale to (`1, 0.7, 1`).

2. Add a **Rigidbody** component to it (**Component | Physics | Rigidbody**). Set the **Mass** property to `0.1`, uncheck **Use Gravity**, open the **Constraints** section, and check **Freeze Position Y** and **Freeze Rotation X**, **Y** and **Z**.

3. Make a new dark grey (`65, 60, 60`) material (**Assets | Create | Material**) called **PuckMaterial** and assign it to the puck's **Mesh Renderer**.

4. Now that the puck is all set, we will make the mallet push it. Go to the mallet's **Move** state in FSM and add an action called **Collision Event** (under Physics) to it. Set the **Collision** property to **On Controller Collider Hit**.

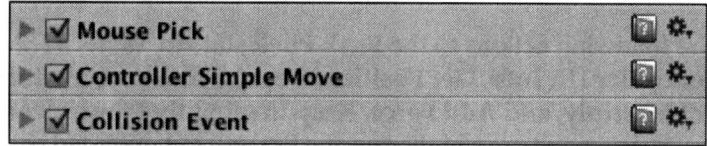

5. Open **TagManager** by selecting the **Puck** game object and choosing **Add Tag...** from the **Tag** drop-down menu in **Inspector**. Create a tag called **Puck** by adding a new tag the same way you did with a layer for the background. Tags are situated near the top of **TagManager**. You can have as many as you want if you modify the **Size** variable. Set the **Puck** game object's tag to **Puck**.

6. Go back to the **Move** state in Mallet's FSM. Set the **Collide Tag** property of the **Collision Event** action to **Puck**.

7. Open the **Events** tab in the **playMaker** panel, enter `Push` in the **Add Event** field near the bottom of the tab, and press *Return* on your keyboard.

8. Open the **State** tab again and set the **Send Event** property of the **Collision Event** action to **Push**.

Components and State Machines

9. Now we have to tell the FSM what will happen once the event is called. Create a new state in the Mallet's FSM by right-clicking anywhere in the FSM view and selecting **Add State** from the context menu. Name the new state Push Puck. Right-click on the **Move** state in the FSM view and select **Add Transition | Push** from the contextual menu. A new light label saying **Push** should appear below the **Move** state. Click on it and drag the line that appears to the **Push Puck** state. This line is the transition that will happen once the **Push** event is called in the **Move** state. Add a **FINISHED** event to the **Push Puck** state the same way. You do not need to create it, because it is a default Playmaker event.

10. Make a transition from the **FINISHED** event to the **Move** state to make sure that when the puck is pushed the mallet will remain under the player's control. The following figure shows what your FSM is supposed to look like:

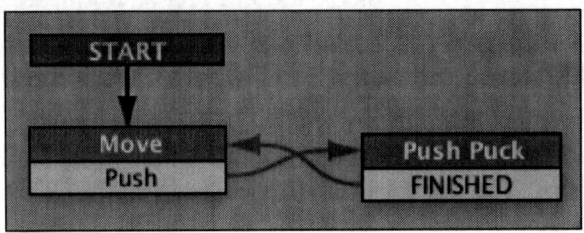

11. Add the following actions to the **Push Puck** state in Mallet's FSM one-by-one: **Get Controller Hit Info**, **Get Position**, **Vector3 Subtract**, **Vector3 Normalize**, **Vector3 Multiply**, and **Add Force**. Keep in mind that the order of the actions matters, because the ones higher on the list will get executed earlier. The following screenshot shows the correct order of the actions.

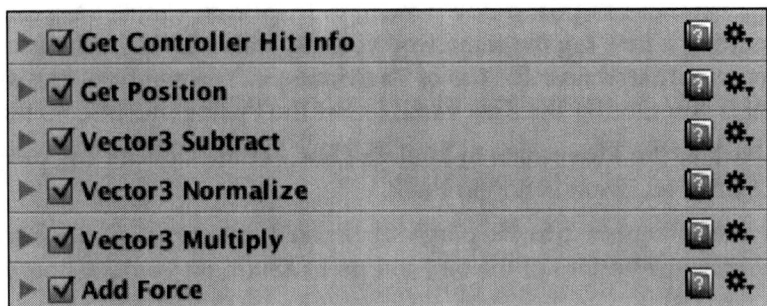

12. Create the following variables using the **Variables** tab of the **playMaker** panel: **hitPos (Vector3)**, **pushDir (Vector3)**, **pushMag (Float)**. Select **pushMag** and set its **Float Value** to 20. This value will determine how hard the mallet pushes the puck.

13. Back in the **State** tab, set the **Contact Point** property of **Get Controller Hit Info** action to **hitPos**.
14. Drag the **Puck** game object from **Hierarchy** to the **Game Object** slot of the **Get Position** action, then set **Vector** to **pushDir**.
15. In **Vector3 Subtract** action, set **Vector3 Variable** to `pushDir`. Click on the small option (🔲) icon next to **Subtract Vector**. This will allow you to pick a variable from the list instead of using a numeric value. Set **Subtract Vector** to `hitPos`.
16. In **Vector3 Normalize** action, set **Vector3 Variable** to **pushDir**.
17. In **Vector3 Multiply** action, set **Vector3 Variable** to **pushDir** and **Multiply By** to **pushMag**. Click on the small option icon to show the FSM variables if needed.
18. Finally, in **Add Force**, set the **Game Object** property to **Specify Game Object** and drag the **Puck** game object into the slot that will appear below. Set **Vector** to **pushDir**. Click on the option icons next to **X**, **Y**, and **Z** and leave them at **None** to make sure they are not reset to 0 and are simply not assigned instead. Click the small option icon to show the **None** option if needed. Then set **Space** to **World**.

Your puck should now become interactive if you click on play and make the Mallet collide with it. I realize that the last bit was a lot of actions at once, so we will discuss what exactly happens in those actions in the next chapter. This is an example of some complex logic that we will look into when we talk more about game mechanics. For now consider it an exercise to familiarize yourself with actions and variables and the way they are added and assigned in the **playMaker** panel.

As another exercise, save your scene, create a few new game objects with FSMs, and try to experiment with different actions and variables, see how they are added and assigned. Don't worry if your actions do not do much. Try to familiarize yourself with the Playmaker interface and remember how to add, move, and remove actions, create new variables and events, and assign them.

Once you feel like you are comfortable with these actions, you can delete the objects you used for practice or simply reload the scene without saving it by double-clicking the `Scene1` file in the **Project** panel.

Summary

In this chapter, we discussed the project structure in Unity: scenes, game objects, components, and properties. We also took a closer look at the Playmaker interface: actions, events, variables, and transitions. You took the first step in creating an air hockey game by implementing a real game mechanic—a mallet that is moved with the mouse and a puck that is pushed when the mallet touches it. In the next chapter, we will add even more game mechanics, explain the ones already implemented in more detail, and try to make the game more fun and pretty.

4
Creating Your First Game

In *Chapter 3*, *Components and State Machines*, you made your first game mechanic for the air hockey game, which we are going to keep improving for the rest of this book. You made a puck and a mallet that is controlled using the mouse pointer and pushes the puck. The pushing mechanic was rather complex and requires some in-depth analysis, which will be the first thing we talk about in this chapter. This chapter is going to cover the following topics:

- Using vector geometry and physics
- Win/lose conditions
- Creating artificial intelligence
- Playmaker debugging

In the end, I will give you a couple of exercises that you will be able to complete with skills and knowledge you will have acquired by the end of this chapter, as well as some advice on how to look for answers to your questions if you have any.

Using Vector geometry and physics

If you are anything like me, you found the title of this section intimidating. However, before you decide to skip it or start looking for a new book about Unity, I assure you that it will not expose you to a single mathematical formula. Instead, it will use the Playmaker actions and explain what each of them does, which, in turn, will lead us to a conclusion about the science behind it.

Practically no 3D video game is possible without vector geometry and physics of some kind, and naturally both are instrumental in explaining how the mallet-puck interaction works in your new air hockey game.

Creating Your First Game

To begin, let us select the **Push Puck** state in the Mallet FSM by clicking on it in the FSM view of the **playMaker** panel and open the **Variables** tab on the right. There are three variables of type **Vector3** and one of type **Float** in the list. The following variables are of interest to us, since they are used for the calculation of push force and direction:

- **hitPos** is a **Vector3** variable in which we store the **X**, **Y**, and **Z** coordinates of the collision point between the mallet and the puck
- **pushDir** is a **Vector3** variable we store the **X**, **Y**, and **Z** direction in which the puck is going to be pushed when it collides with the mallet
- **pushMag** is a **Float** variable that is currently equal to 20 and corresponds to the magnitude of the push

To understand how things work in video games, you will have to be comfortable using **Vector3** variables, because much of everything you will do is going to happen in 3D space. Each **Transform** component has three **Vector3** properties: **Position**, **Rotation**, and **Scale**, each of which has its own **X**, **Y**, and **Z** values.

Each point in 3D space has coordinates that can be written down in the form of three **Float** variables: a position on the X axis, a position on the Y axis, and a position on the Z axis. A **Vector3** variable can store these three position values at the same time.

You can perform various actions over **Vector3**, you can add it to another vector, you can multiply it by a float (or an integer), you can store its **X**, **Y**, and **Z** in separate **Float** variables or write separate float values into its **X**, **Y**, and **Z**. Most of these actions are under the **Vector3** category of the **Actions** panel.

The first action that we use is called **Get Controller Hit Info**, and it gets the position of the last collision that happened to a game object. If you look at the **Collision Event** action in the **Move** state that triggers the **Push** event, you will see that this only happens when the mallet collides with the puck, so we do not have to worry about weeding out false collisions once we are already in the **Push Puck** state. All we have to do is save the contact point in a variable, which is exactly what happens.

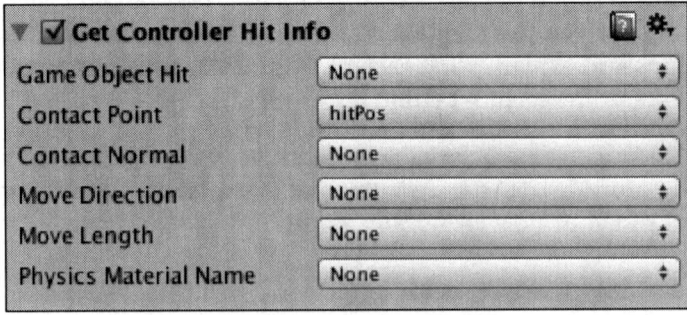

Next, we simply get the current position of the mallet and store it in the **pushDir** variable, for the time being using the **GetPosition** action. This variable is called **pushDir**, because later it will contain the direction in which the mallet will be pushed. We get this position simply by accessing the **Position** property of the mallet's **Transform** component.

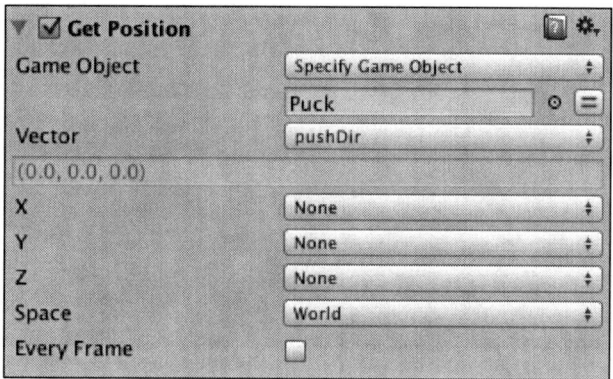

If these are all positions, how do you get a direction? What is a direction and how can you write it down in **Vector3**? The answer is quite simple. A direction is the relative position of one point with respect to another point in space, which is another way of saying that it is the difference between **Position A** and **Position B**. The following figure shows two points and their relative directions.

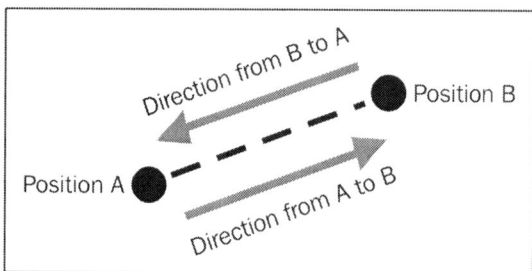

So, in order to find the direction in which point B lies in relation to point A, you will have to subtract the position of point B from the position of point A. Then you need to normalize the result, which means writing it down as a **Vector3** variable that has its **X**, **Y**, and **Z** properties as numbers between 0 and 1 (that is, without a magnitude).

Creating Your First Game

For example, if the original result of subtraction was (-1, 27, 350), the normalized vector of direction will be (-0.00284867, 0.076914, 0.997034), and the best part of it is that you do not need to know how this happens, because there is a Playmaker action that does it automatically for you. The following screenshot shows the two actions that are used to get the direction from the center of the mallet to the hit point:

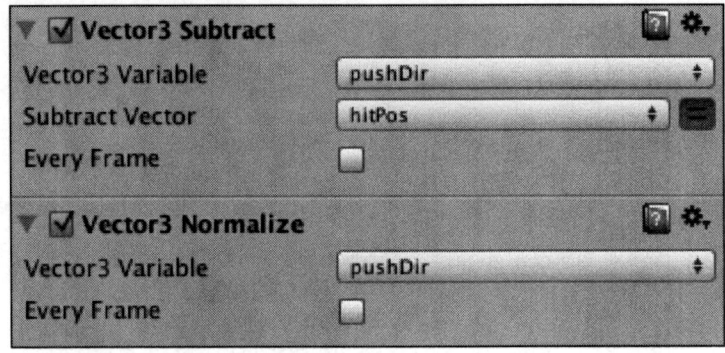

Let us go through the things we have covered so far:

- We need the position of the mallet, because this is where we are going to push the puck from
- We need the point of the impact between the mallet and the puck in order to find where the puck lies in space in relation to the mallet when the mallet hits it
- Both of these values are saved as **Vector3** variables, each of which contains an **X**, **Y**, and **Z** position
- We can find out in which direction the puck lies in relation to the mallet by subtracting the position of the impact from the position of the mallet and normalizing the resulting vector, that is, writing down its **X**, **Y**, and **Z** properties as numbers between 0 and 1

Now that we know how to find the direction in which the puck lies in relation to the mallet, we want to push it in that direction, so this is exactly what we are going to do. However, we cannot just assign the direction vector as the puck's velocity, because the direction vector does not have a magnitude, which means that the velocity of the puck will be way smaller than we want it to be.

In order to control the force with which the puck is being pushed, we have to multiply the direction by a magnitude, which is stored in the **pushMag** variable. This variable determines how fast the puck will move in the opposite direction once it meets the mallet.

> If you assign **pushMag** a negative value, the puck will be pushed towards the mallet every time it collides with it, which, in turn, means that it will stick to it. This too can be a useful game mechanic, albeit not in this case.

The following screenshot shows the **Vector3 Multiply** action that multiplies the **pushDir** direction vector by **pushMag** magnitude as well as the **Add Force** action that applies the force to the puck at the impact point.

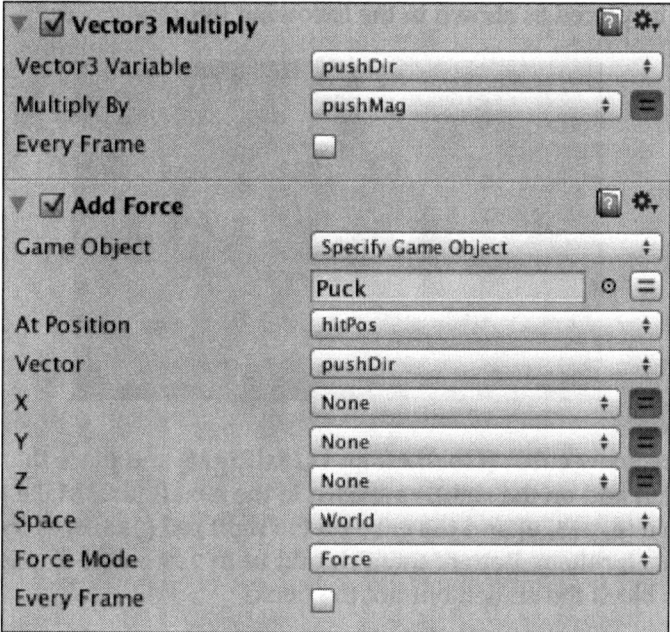

Win/Lose conditions

While there are games where win/lose conditions are not necessary, air hockey is definitely not one of them. In classic air hockey, there are two goal slots on the opposite sides of the table. If the puck gets into the goal of player 1, then player 2 gets a point and vice versa. The game ends when one of the players has 7 points.

There is the short-term win condition (score once) and the long-term win condition (score seven times before your opponent does). We will only implement the short-term win condition, although you are highly encouraged to try and implement the long-term one once you are done with this chapter.

Creating Your First Game

Before we start implementing the win/lose conditions, let us make sure that the puck cannot get stuck in the corner, because this kind of behavior will prevent the win/lose condition from being triggered. Make four new walls, rotate them 45 degrees on the Y axis, and place them in the corners so as to get rid of the straight angles there, as shown in the next figure. This should solve the problem.

Now that this is taken care of, let us make the goal slots. Change the puck's **Scale** property to (1, 0.7, 1) and place it in (-3, 0.3, 0).

1. Make one more wall on the left and one more wall on the right. The walls should be placed as shown in the following figure:

   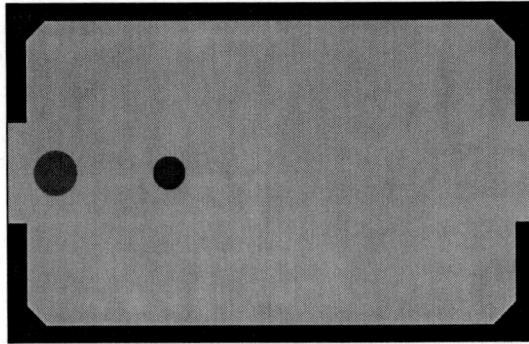

2. Make two new cubes (**GoalLeft** and **GoalRight**) and place them in the gaps on the left and on the right, as shown in the next figure. Make the cube on the left green (0, 255, 0) and the cube on the right red (255, 0, 0) by making new materials for them. Both of them should be in 2.5 on the Y axis. These are there to block the mallet, but not the puck.

3. Make two more cubes. Call them GoalTriggerLeft and GoalTriggerRight. Place them just behind the game field on either side of the table. These objects will act as triggers to detect which goal the puck has scored. Check the **Is Trigger** property of these game objects' **Box Collider** component. This property of the collider component makes sure that the object does not do any physics collisions (as opposed to the puck or the walls), but instead acts as a trigger, detecting when rigidbodies enter, stay inside, and exit it. These objects are the actual goals that will trigger the win/lose conditions.

4. Your **Scene** view should look something like the following screenshot at this point:

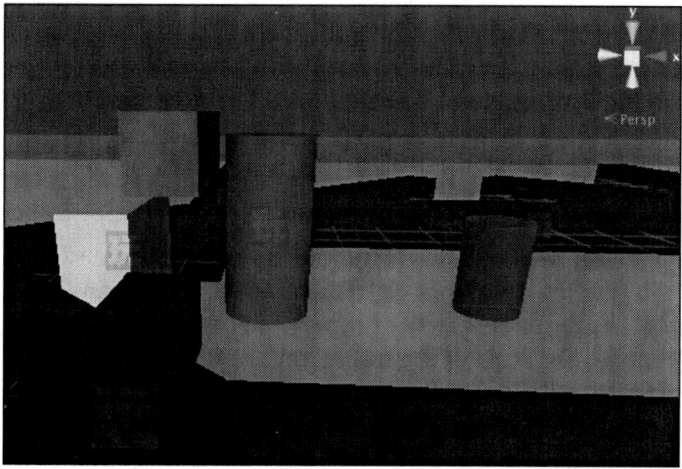

5. Select the **GoalTriggerLeft** game object and add an FSM to it. Make two states and rename **State1** to `Scored` and **State2** to `LoadLevel`.

6. Right-click the **Scored** state and go to **Add Transition** | **System Events** | **TRIGGER ENTER** from the contextual menu.

7. Make a transition from **TRIGGER ENTER** to **LoadLevel**. When something enters the trigger (and it should only be the puck, because of the way things are placed in the scene), this event will get called, and the transition will be made.

8. Select the **LoadLevel** state and add a **Load Level** action to it. It should be located under the **Level** category.

9. In the **Level Name** property of the **Load Level** action, type the name of your game scene. It should be called `Scene1` if you haven't changed anything. To make sure, look at the top of the **Unity Editor** window. It always says `[SceneName].unity - [ProjectName] - [Platform]`, where the things in the brackets are **Scene1**, **UPMTutorial**, and **Web Player** for me, but can differ for you.

10. Do the same thing for **GoalTriggerRight**. For now, keep the FSM exactly the same.

Now, we can add some finishing touches to our scene by importing a 3D model:

1. Make sure that you have downloaded the project archive from the Packt Publishing website. If you haven't, do it now and unpack the archive.

Creating Your First Game

2. Right-click in the empty space under the file list in the **Project** panel and select **Import New Asset...** from the contextual menu. A file browser should pop up.

3. Locate the `WallVisual.fbx` file in the `UnityPlaymakerTutorial` directory and click on **Import**. The file browser will close and a `WallVisual` file will appear in the **Project** panel. Create a `Models` folder and drag it there.

4. Select the `WallVisual` file and have a look at **Inspector**. There are three tabs in this **Inspector**: **Model, Rig,** and **Animations**. These are all responsible for changing import settings of your model.

5. Since the model that we have imported is not an animated one, only the **Model** tab is of interest to us. Set **Scale Factor** to `1.05` and uncheck **Import Materials**. Leave the rest of the properties at their default values. **Scale Factor** changes the scale of the model on import, meaning that the **Transform Scale** property will be equal to (1, 1, 1) while the actual size in 3D space may change. This is needed because the working scale in the 3D modeling software (such as Maya or 3DS Max) may differ from that in Unity. To make the model appear bigger, increase the scale factor. See the following screenshot to confirm that your import settings are set correctly:

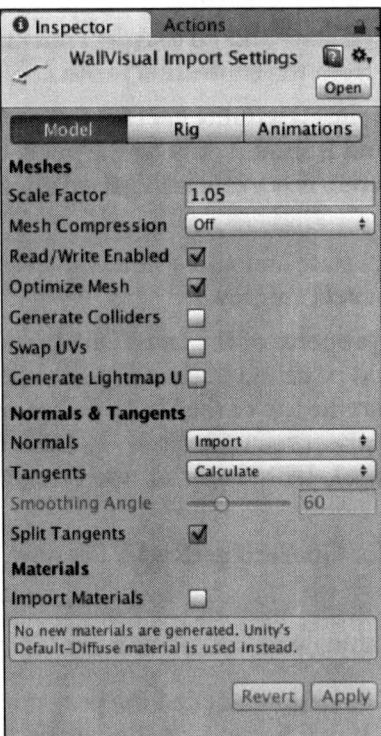

Chapter 4

6. Drag **WallVisual** into **Hierarchy** twice. Position the first instance in (0, 0.5, -3.5) and the second one in (0, 0.5, 3.5). Set the first one's **Rotation** to (0, 0, 0) and the second one's to (0, 180, 0).

> The difference between a prefab and an imported model is that you cannot apply the changes that you made to one of the instances. You also cannot add or remove any components from the model. You can make a prefab from one of the instances of the model to be able to do that.

7. Set the material of both **WallVisual** game objects to **WallMaterial** that you created previously to be used on walls. Select all of the **Wall** objects and deactivate their **Mesh Renderer** components. The following figure shows what you should see in the **Game** view if you did everything right:

Now, when you hit play, you should be able to score in both goals. Doing so will reload the currently loaded level. We also made sure that the puck does not get stuck in the corners of the table and imported a model that covers our cubic walls and makes the game look more like an actual air hockey table. This means that the game is finally playable, if, admittedly, not very fun yet.

Creating artificial intelligence

Having an **artificial intelligence** (**AI**) in the game, even a really simple one, will definitely make it more challenging and fun, so let us get to it with no further delay.

Here is how our AI is going to work: it is going to constantly try and move to the point on the right side of the puck, pushing it to the left upon collision. We will keep the same collision logic that we use for the player's mallet in order to keep the game fair. In order to make sure that the AI does not get stuck in a wall while pushing directly to the left, we will make adjustments to the direction based on the current position of the mallet. This way, the AI will appear to aim at the player's goal slot.

Follow the given steps to implement the AI:

1. Duplicate the **Mallet** game object by selecting it in **Hierarchy** and pressing *command* + *D* (*Ctrl* + *D* in Windows).
2. Move the copy to the right side of the table and put it next to the red goal.
3. Name the original mallet on the left `MalletLeft`, and the copy on the right `MalletRight`.
4. Make a new red material for **MalletRight** and assign it to it.
5. Put both mallets on a new layer called **Player** using the **TagManager** menu accessible from **Inspector**.
6. In the main menu, go to **Edit | Project Settings | Physics**. You will see a matrix of checkboxes with names of layers written horizontally and vertically next to each row and column in the **Inspector** panel.
7. Find the intersection between **Player** horizontally and **Player** vertically and uncheck that box. Make sure that the rest of the boxes stay checked. This matrix determines which layers can interact with each other and with themselves, so if you accidentally uncheck something else, such as **Default/Player** or **Default/Default**, the puck may no longer collide with the goal triggers and the mallets may stop colliding with the walls.
8. Select the **MalletRight** game object. In **Inspector**, remove the **Character Controller** component and add **Capsule Collider**. Add a **Rigidbody** component. Set **Freeze Rotation** on the **Rigidbody** component to X, Y and Z. If you don't, the red mallet will fall when you press play. **Rigidbody** is the component responsible for physics interactions.
9. In the FSM view of the **playMaker** panel, select the **Move** state. It is here that we are going to set up the AI.

10. Remove all the actions except **Collision Event**. You can select multiple actions at the same time by *Shift*-clicking their headers. Open the **Actions** panel and add the following actions to the state, keeping in mind that the order of the actions matters, and moving **Collision Event** to the very bottom: **Get Property, Get Property, Get Property, Float Multiply, Float Add, Float Add, Set Vector3 XYZ**, and **Move Towards**. The following screenshot shows the exact order of the actions that you should have in the **Move** state of the FSM of **MalletRight**.

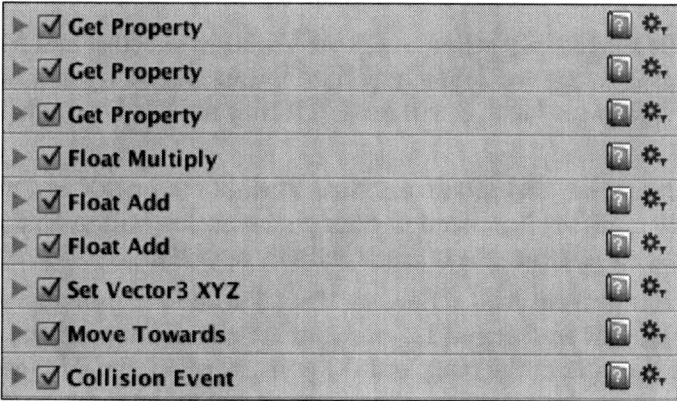

11. In the **Events** tab, add a new event, calling it `Return`.
12. Open the **Variables** tab and add/remove variables until you have the variables shown in the following screenshot:

Name	Used	Type
hitPos	3	Vector3
offset	3	Float
puckX	3	Float
puckZ	3	Float
pushDir	5	Vector3
pushMag	1	Float
targetPos	2	Vector3

13. These are the variables used for collision calculations that were left from before, and some new ones used for the simple AI behavior that we discussed earlier.

14. Go back to the **State** tab and open the first **Get Property** action. Drag and drop the **Puck** game object into **Target Object**, and set **Property** to **transform | position | x** and **Store Float** to **puckX**. Check **Every Frame**. In fact, check **Every Frame** every time you see this checkbox in this state.

15. Do the same for the second **Get Property** tab, but choose z instead of x and **puckZ** instead of **puckX**. These actions are used to retrieve the position of the puck on the two axes that matter to us.

16. Open the third **Get Property** action and drag **MalletRight** into its **Target Object** property; store its Z position in the offset variable.

17. In the **Float Multiply** action, set **Float Variable** to **offset** and **Multiply By** to 0.2. This is where we define how hard the AI should try to aim the player's goal. If it tries too hard, it will miss. If it tries not hard enough, it will miss as well.

18. In the first **Float Add** action, set **Float Variable** to **puckX** and the **Add** property to **offset**. You need to click on the option button on the right to do that. This is where the offset is actually applied.

19. In the second **Float Add** action, set **Float Variable** to **puckZ**, and **Add** to 0.9. This value can be changed as you want later. It defines the distance between the actual center of the puck and the point to which the AI is going to move. It is very important that the AI aim somewhat to the right, because otherwise it will never be able to hit the player's goal.

20. In **Set Vector3 XYZ**, set **Vector3 Variable** to **targetPos**, X to **puckX**, and Z to **puckZ**. Make sure that **Y** is set to **None**. This is where we define the actual position where the AI is going to try and go in the current frame.

21. **Move Towards** is the action that applies movement to the AI. Set **Target Position** to **targetPos**, **Max Speed** to 5, **Finish Distance** to 0.15, and **Finish Event** to **Return**.

22. Finally, open **Collision Event** and change its **Collision** property to **On Collision Stay**; leaving everything else intact.

23. Now you might have an error in the **Move Towards** action. That would be because there is no transition from the **Return** event. Right-click the **Move** state in the FSM view and add a transition from the **Return** event to **Move**. Yes, this is a state that loops on itself. The following figure shows the layout that you should see in the FSM view of **MalletRight** now.

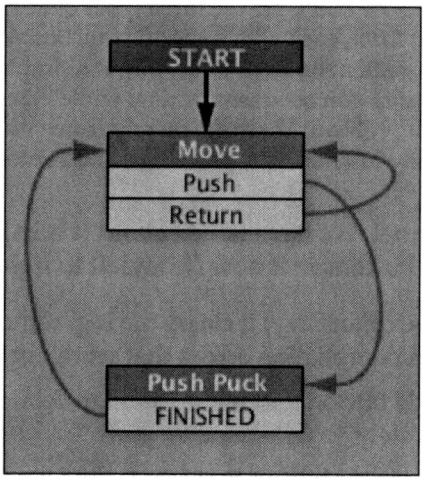

If you click on the play button right now, the AI should be completely functional and, in fact, quite strong. Now, there are ways of improving it that will be discussed in the *Exercises* section of this chapter, but it should be enough to have a good bit of fun with the game debugging in Playmaker.

Now that you have a player controller, a win/lose condition, and a functional AI in the game, it begins to get quite big, and if you want to add anything to it or if something goes wrong, you will be hard-pressed to know what exactly is going on in your actions in real time. This is what debugging is for: it is a diagnosis tool that lets you get additional information about your game or its specific systems that you can later use in order to fix something.

Let us look at an example. Select **MalletLeft** and open its **Move** state in the FSM view of the **playMaker** panel. If you look at the bottom of the **State** tab, you will see two checkboxes there: **Debug** and **Hide Unused**. The first one shows you the values of all your properties at all time, while the second one hides the unused ones. Check both of them and, keeping **MalletLeft** selected, press the play button.

As you move the mallet around, observe the numbers that change under all the properties of the actions. When you implement a new gameplay feature, you will want to know in what range values change, and if they do at all.

Creating Your First Game

You can also use the **Console** panel for debugging some things. Uncheck both **Debug** and **Hide Unused**, and then open the **Push Puck** state of the same FSM. Add a **Debug Log** action (under the **Debug** category) to the very top of it. Set **Log Level** to **Warning** and write Hit! in the text field.

> You should know that there are three types of debug logs: *Info*, *Warning*, and *Error*, each with a specific function. Warning is there to attract your attention to an issue, Info is a simple message that provides information about something, while Error lets you know that there is a problem. These are merely conventions, but you will see some Unity internal Info, Warnings, and Errors that follow them.

Now open the **Console** panel. We have talked about it briefly before, but let us have a detailed look at various buttons in it now (from left to right).

- **Clear** is quite self-explanatory; it clears the log, removing all the messages from it, apart from compilation errors that were not fixed
- **Collapse** is a toggle button that makes similar debug messages appear in the same line or separately
- **Clear on Play** is a toggle button that forces the **Console** to clear the log when you press play.
- **Error Pause** automatically pauses the game when there is an error to give you a better look at it.

Finally, the three toggle buttons on the right are filters for **Console** that let you focus on different types of debug messages: Info, Warning, and Error.

If you press play now and hit the puck with your mallet, a message with a yellow triangle should appear in Console saying something like **MalletLeft : FSM : Push Puck : DebugLog : Hit!** You might also have several of them. Stop the game and see what happens when you switch **Collapse** on and off and toggle the Warning filter. If you press play now and hit the puck with your mallet, a message with a yellow triangle should appear in Console saying something like **MalletLeft : FSM : Push Puck : DebugLog : Hit!** You might also have several of them. Stop the game and see what happens when you switch **Collapse** on and off and toggle the Warning filter. You might also have several of them, as shown in the following screenshot:

You can also debug variable values in the same way. Open **playMaker**, remove the **Debug Log** action, and put a **Debug Vector3** action right after **Get Controller Hit Info**, setting the **Log Level** to **Error** and **Vector3 Variable** to **hitPos**. Then open **Console** and test the game again, pushing the puck with your mallet. You should see red error messages appear in **Console** now. If you have **Error Pause** toggled, the game will pause and the **Console** panel will be revealed to show you the errors.

You can achieve a similar effect by using something called breakpoints. Get rid of the **Debug Vector3** action in the **Push Puck** state of the FSM of **MalletLeft**, then right-click on the **Push Puck** state in the FSM view and select **Toggle Breakpoint** from the contextual menu. A red line will appear next to the state's name in the FSM view.

Now, if you press play and touch the puck with your mallet, the game will stop the same way it did when you used an **Error Debug** log and the **Error Pause** toggle in **Console**, except this time the pause will be triggered by Playmaker. A red circle with the name of the breakpoint's state will appear in the FSM view. The following screenshot shows what it is supposed to look like:

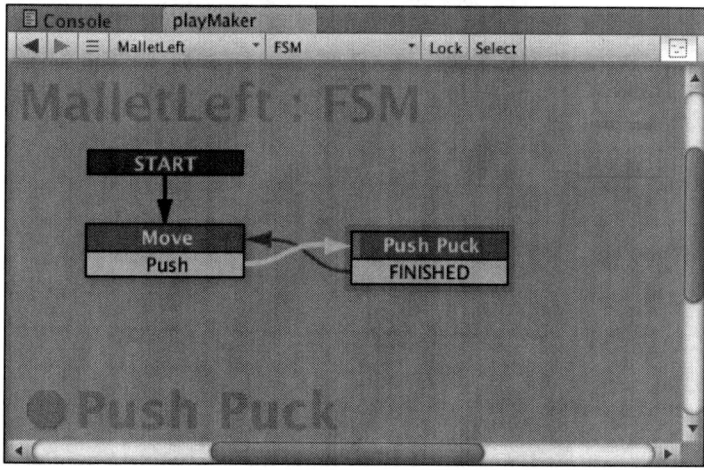

Note that the transition arrow from the **Push** event to the **Push Puck** state became yellow. This means that the breakpoint was triggered after this particular transition and not something else.

You can unpause the game when it was paused because of a breakpoint, but it will be paused all over again if this or another breakpoint gets triggered. You can remove the breakpoint by right-clicking the state with a breakpoint and selecting **Toggle Breakpoint** from the contextual menu.

Creating Your First Game

Another useful debugging tool is step-by-step execution. When the game is paused (including when it was paused because of breakpoints or **Error Pause**), you can press the next step ( ) button in the toolbar or on the bottom of the **playMaker** panel. This will execute the next frame of the game. As you already know, some actions are executed in every frame so, using the **Debug** checkbox on the bottom of the **State** tab in the **playMaker** panel, you can see the exact values of each parameter of each action in any particular frame. You can press the next step button as you want to observe changes. When you are done debugging, just unpause or stop the game.

The final debug tool that we are going to talk about is the Playmaker **FSM Log** panel that lets you see everything that happens to your objects that are under Playmaker control. You can open it by pressing the **Debug** button on the bottom of the **playMaker** panel next to the play/pause/next step buttons, then select **Open Log Window** from the drop-down menu. The following screenshot shows the **FSM Log** panel in action:

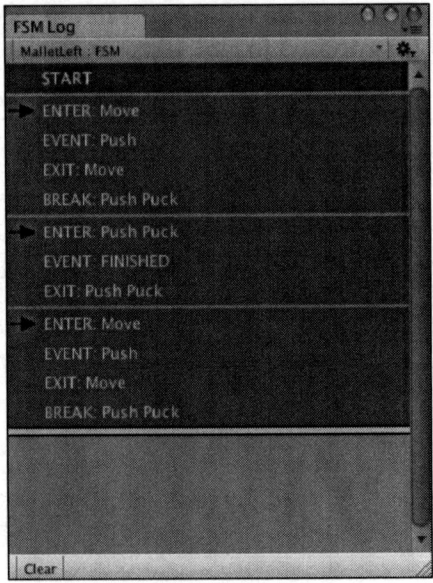

It might be a good idea to keep this log handy, so you could attach it as the second panel to the same area of the screen as **Hierarchy** or **Project**.

Exercises

There are some exercises that I would like to suggest that you try doing before you move on to the next chapters, which cover more advanced topics. You already know the basics of Unity and Playmaker—enough to make your game better or make a completely new one from scratch. Doing these exercises will improve your skills and help consolidate the new information that you have been exposed to in this book. Exercises are sorted by difficulty, from the easiest to the hardest one:

1. Debug log all the important events in the game, including puck hits, goal hits, and wall collisions for both mallets.

2. Hit sounds: Your `Wall` prefab has a FSM. Use it to play some sounds when a mallet and/or a puck hits the wall. `Freesound.org` is a good resource for free sound effects. If you are more into retro sounds, try `bfxr.net`.

3. Multiple levels: Try making multiple levels with obstacles/additional walls in the middle. You can just duplicate them all over the place and then, when the round is over, move on to the next level.

4. By now you have probably encountered a situation where the puck falls off of the table, and you are forced to restart the game using the play button. This is annoying for other players as well! You could try changing the table set up, detecting the puck position, or some other way of fixing this.

> When you are working on this, think about the way goal triggers work, or be creative and come up with your own solution.

5. You know how to manipulate the **Scene** view and make new materials for objects, and you also know how to change the size and the projection of the camera. You can make your game much prettier if you come up with a beautiful color scheme and/or camera projection/orientation.

6. By now you have probably started wondering whether mouse controls are the best solution for this game. This is a perfectly valid question, and you should make this decision yourself. You will never know for sure until you try different ones, so take a look at the **Input** category in the **Actions** panel.

7. If you manage to implement keyboard controls, why not go a step further and make a level where instead of competing with an AI opponent you could play with your friend or family member while sitting at the same computer?

8. Have a close look at states and actions that control the AI. Try modifying some of the properties there or even replacing actions themselves in order to make the AI more intelligent and life-like. You could try and make the AI alternate its behavior based on the position of the puck by going back to its own goal slot in order to protect it. You can also try and figure out a way to stop the AI from being pushed backwards whenever the player pushes the puck that the AI is trying to push itself.

> In order to do this, you will need to add a Playmaker variable to the puck and then use one of the **Get FSM** actions under the **StateMachine** category.

9. Introduce a new game mechanic to the game: how about rounds of seven games instead of one? Or power-ups? Or limiting the mallets to their side of the table? You choose, you can do them all if you like.

Before you take up any of these challenges, you should know about some of the useful Unity and Playmaker online resources that can help you find answers to some, if not all, of the questions. You can be sure that questions will inevitably appear when you start implementing something on your own.

- **Unity answers**: `http://answers.unity3d.com/`
- **Unity wiki**: `http://wiki.unity3d.com/`
- **Unity forum**: `http://forum.unity3d.com/`
- **Unity documentation**: `http://unity3d.com/learn/documentation`
- **Playmaker manual**: `https://hutonggames.fogbugz.com/`
- **Playmaker forums**: `http://hutonggames.com/playmakerforum/`

On Unity answers and the Unity forums, you should not hesitate to ask questions; the Unity community is very active, and there are chances that your problem will be solved in a matter of minutes. Just make sure you explain it well. But before asking, I strongly advise you to use the search option first, since there is a good chance that most of the problems that you might encounter have already been solved.

Summary

In this chapter, you learned the fundamentals of game development with Unity and Playmaker. You now know how to make objects, have them interact, make them respond to input, and even move on their own based on your algorithm. On top of that, you now know the fundamentals of vector geometry that you are going to use in most of the games you will make.

The next chapter is about programming. You will learn how to code your own Unity component and then make it into a Playmaker action. We will also demonstrate that Playmaker is essentially visual programming that uses logic very similar to that of conventional scripts.

5
Scripting and Custom Actions

In previous chapters, you learned how to make a game using Playmaker's in-built actions. Unfortunately, their capabilities are limited, and sooner or later you will find yourself in need of something that Playmaker does not know how to do out-of-the-box. In this case, you can try and find a ready-made solution on the Internet, but to make sure that there is an answer to every one of your questions, you will certainly have to learn how to write scripts. These are the topics that we will discuss in this chapter:

- Programming in Unity JavaScript (sometimes also called UnityScript) and C#
- Common Unity classes, variables, and functions
- Writing a script and using it as component
- Transforming a script into a Playmaker action

Writing a Unity Script

Explaining how programming works in general is beyond the scope of this book, so I am going to assume that you already know what variables, functions, classes, and operators are. If, however, you do not know these things, it should not take you too long to pick up the basics using either Code Academy (http://www.codecademy.com/tracks/javascript) or Unity's own starting level tutorials (http://unity3d.com/learn/tutorials/modules/beginner/scripting).

We are going to start with **JavaScript (JS)** in this section, because it is much simpler to use and does not require any understanding of object-oriented programming beyond the component-based approach to development that we already discussed in *Chapter 3, Components and State Machines*. Besides, you will end up writing significantly less code.

Scripting and Custom Actions

Both JS and C# use the same Unity classes and functions, and the difference in syntax is not very significant at all. However, for more complex things it is generally a good idea to use C# (for one thing, it is currently impossible to write a Playmaker action in JavaScript). We will start with a JS script and then translate it into C#, explaining the differences. You can later choose whichever language works better for you.

We are going to create a script that replaces all the Playmaker actions in the **Push Puck** state of both mallets' FSMs. When you see that you have to make a chain of five or more actions, it is generally easier to combine them in a single custom action, especially if you are planning to use this compound action on multiple objects.

Let us start by creating a new script. First of all, create a new folder named `Scripts` using the **Project** panel. Then, right-click on the newly created folder and navigate to **Create | Javascript**. Name the file `PushPuck`. Double-click on the file. The standard Unity programming environment, MonoDevelop, should open. Select everything there is in that script and replace it with the following code:

```
// Automatically added, compiler =directive
// that makes JavaScript more explicit
#pragma strict

// Global variables available from Inspector
var pushMag : float = 20f;

var collisionTag : String = String.Empty;

// Function that will detect the collision with
// controller and apply force in point of the collision
function OnControllerColliderHit (hit : ControllerColliderHit)
{
  if (hit.gameObject.tag == collisionTag)
  {
    // Get the position of the object we collided with
    var hitObjectPos : Vector3 = hit.transform.position;

    // Get the position of the collision
    var hitPointPos : Vector3 = hit.point;

    // Calculate the direction of the force,
    // multiply it by magnitude
    var pushForce : Vector3 = Vector3.Normalize(hitObjectPos -
      hitPointPos) * pushMag;

    // Finally, apply force in position
    hit.rigidbody.AddForceAtPosition(pushForce, hitPointPos);
```

```
        // Print a message in Console saying that
        //the collision did happen and force was indeed applied
        Debug.Log("Detected hit with " + collisionTag +
           ", applying force of " + pushForce + " in " + hitPointPos +
           ".");
    }
}
@script RequireComponent(CharacterController)
```

> You can download the example code files for all Packt Publishing books you have purchased from your account at http://www.packtpub.com. If you purchased this book elsewhere, you can visit http://www.packtpub.com/support and register to have the files e-mailed directly to you.

Press *command* + *S* (*Ctrl* + *S* in Windows) in MonoDevelop to save the changes to the script.

Let us examine this code line-by-line. The first line is #pragma strict. This is a preprocessor directive. If you have some previous programming experience, you have probably seen something similar before. It does not participate in script logic; what it does is make JavaScript more explicit by imposing more strict error handling in the compiler. What it means for you is that you have to explicitly define the types of your variables, which is something you would not normally do in standard JavaScript.

> Another common preprocessor directive for JS is #pragma downcast, which lets you get rid of warnings of implicit downcast if you do not care about them.

After that there are two lines of variable declaration: pushMag and collisionTag are declared as float and String. Once you attach this script to an object, these variables will be displayed in the Inspector, because they are both public and serialized. Since a script in Unity is treated as a component, variables appear as parameters in the Inspector once you attach the script to a game object.

If you want to declare a variable that does not appear in the Inspector, but want other scripts to still have access to it, you should put [System.NonSerialized] before it. If you want to both hide it and close all access to it, you just need to put private before the var keyword. Finally, if you want to expose a private variable in Inspector, you should put [System.SerializableAttribute] before its declaration.

Scripting and Custom Actions

Next goes the function declaration: `function OnControllerColliderHit (hit : ControllerColliderHit)`. `OnControllerColliderHit` is one of the standard Unity functions that are responsible for detecting collisions. Other such functions are `OnCollisionEnter`, `OnCollisionStay`, `OnCollisionExit`, `OnTriggerEnter`, `OnTriggerStay`, and `OnTriggerExit`.

The `OnControllerColliderHit` function gets called automatically if the object that the script is attached to has a Character Controller component and that Character Controller collides with a collider. The `hit` variable of type `ControllerColliderHit` gets assigned and can be used inside the function. By typing `hit` and a dot, one can access all kinds of information about the collision.

For instance, inside the function there is an `if` condition: `if (hit.gameObject.tag == collisionTag)`. We access the `gameObject` that our Character Controller has collided with, using the dot operator, and then we use it again to access that tag in `gameObject`. Then we compare that tag with the `collisionTag` string variable that is assigned in the Inspector. If the tag matches the string we specified, the code inside the curly brackets is executed.

In this script, we reproduced the exact sequence of actions in the **Push Puck** state of the mallets' FSMs. You can consult it for reference. First, we get the position of the puck and store it in a `Vector3` variable called `hitObjectPos`. Then we get the point of the hit and store it in another `Vector3` variable called `hitPointPos`. We then calculate the force of the push in one step instead of three that we used in Playmaker. Finally, the force is applied to the puck's rigidbody.

After that there is a line with `Debug.Log` that prints information about every hit in the Console. You can comment this line out by typing `//` in front of it. Keep it uncommented for now to make sure that the script works.

The very last line of the script is `@script RequireComponent (CharacterController)`. It is there to make sure that there is a Character Controller component attached to the game object that this script is attached to. If you attach this script to a game object that does not have a Character Controller, it will be attached automatically. If you try to remove the Character Controller without removing `PushPuck` first, Unity will display a warning dialog window and not allow you to do it.

Now it is time to see if our newly created script works. Go back to Unity and open the **Console** panel. If there are no red errors, this means that the script was compiled correctly and is ready to be used. If there is some kind of error in a script, double-clicking on it in the Console will open the script in MonoDevelop and direct you to the line where the error has occurred.

If everything is okay, select **MalletLeft**, open the **playMaker** panel and in the **Move** state disable the **Collision Event** action by unchecking the box next to its name. If you start the game now, colliding with the puck will not push it. Now it is time to use our brand-new `PushPuck` script. Drag and drop the `PushPuck` file from the **Project** panel to the **Inspector** panel while having **MalletLeft** selected. It will attach to it as a component. Set its parameters as shown in the following screenshot:

Open the **Console** panel and launch the game. Note how messages appear in the Console every time you hit the puck with your mallet. If you stop the game and double-click on one of the `Debug.Log`s, MonoDevelop will open and point you to the `Debug.Log` line of the `PushPuck` script. Now that you know the script works, you can comment that line out in order to prevent it from spamming the console.

Also, now you can apply it to the AI opponent as well. Remember to deactivate the **Collision Event** action first.

Overview of standard Unity classes

While I am not going to copy the whole Unity Script Reference into this chapter of the book, I would like to list a few important classes and functions that you are going to use quite often.

The most obvious and frequently used standard functions are `Awake`, `Start`, `OnEnable`, `OnDisable`, `Update`, and `FixedUpdate`:

- `Awake` is the first function that is called when a scene is loaded. The `Awake` function can happen only once per scene load. It is generally a good idea to put all initialization code into the `Awake` function.

- `Start` happens after `Awake` and also runs once. Sometimes it is a good idea to put some code into `Awake` and some other code into `Start` in order to make sure that one is executed after the other. When you have an `Awake` function in one script and another `Awake` function in another script, you cannot be sure which one will be executed first. If the order matters, put one of the pieces of code into the `Start` function.

>  There's another way to ensure a correct script execution order. You can decide which script is executed before or after by navigating to **Edit | Project Settings | Script Execution Order** from the main menu and then pressing the plus button in the Inspector, selecting the script whose execution order you would like to define, and then dragging it up or down in the interface. You will notice that the number on the right changes as you drag the script: this number is the script's execution order. You give the script its default execution order by removing it from this list. You can do this by pressing the minus button on the right from its name in the list.

- The `OnEnable` function is a lot like `Start`, except it is called every time the object to which the script is attached is activated, as well as every time the component itself is enabled.
- `OnDisable` is the opposite of `OnEnable`. It is called when the object or the component gets disabled.
- `Update` is called every frame. Most of the games' logic usually happens here.
- `FixedUpdate` is called on physics update, which is generally significantly more frequent than `Update`. All the code that cannot be frame rate dependent (such as, for instance, movement) should be in the `FixedUpdate` function.

Apart from the functions, there are whole classes with their methods and variables that you should absolutely know about when programming in Unity. It is hard to emphasize something in particular, and you really should just go through all the major classes listed in the Scripting Reference (http://docs.unity3d.com/Documentation/ScriptReference/). There are really a lot of classes, and there is hardly anyone who knows what all of them do, but we are going to go through a few that you should look at first thing: `Mathf`, `Vector3`, `Color`, `Input`, `GameObject`, `Transform`, `Renderer`, `Material`, `Collision`, `Collider`, and of course `Object`, `Behaviour`, `Component`, and `MonoBehaviour`.

The last four classes are especially important, since they include things that you are going to use every time you write a script in Unity, including functions like `Update`, `Destroy`, `GetComponent`, and `Start`, as well as variables such as `enabled`, `name`, `layer`, and `tag`. Try to read descriptions of these classes and their functions and variables very carefully, and look at the basic examples the documentation offers with them.

Creating a Playmaker action

It is time to translate our script to C#. Create a new C# script the same way you created the JS one. Call it `PushPuckAction`. Open the script and find the line starting with the `public class` keywords. Make sure that the name of the class is the same as the name of the script, then press *command + S* (*Ctrl + S* in Windows) to save your changes if you made any.

As you can see, the default template for a C# script looks different from that of JS. This is because more things are shown to you. For instance, in JS it is implied that everything inside a script is, in fact, in a class with the same name, but you do not see the class declaration anywhere. Component classes in Unity have to inherit from MonoBehaviour, and it is shown in C#, while JS hides it from you. Then you have the two lines with the `using` keyword. All JS scripts use these namespaces, but JS hides it from you as well. The following script is the same one that we had before, but this time translated to C#. Replace the template with it.

```csharp
using UnityEngine;
using System.Collections;
[RequireComponent (typeof (CharacterController))]

public class PushPuckAction : MonoBehaviour
{
  // Global variables available from Inspector
  public float pushMag = 20f;

  public string collisionTag = string.Empty;

  // Function that will detect the collision with
  // controller and apply force in point of the collision
  void OnControllerColliderHit (ControllerColliderHit hit)
  {
    if (hit.gameObject.tag == collisionTag)
    {
      // Get the position of the object we collided with
      Vector3 hitObjectPos = hit.transform.position;

      // Get the position of the collision
      Vector3 hitPointPos = hit.point;

      // Calculate the direction of the force,
      // multiply it by magnitude
      Vector3 pushForce = Vector3.Normalize(hitObjectPos -
        hitPointPos) * pushMag;
```

Scripting and Custom Actions

```
            // Finally, apply force in position
            hit.rigidbody.AddForceAtPosition(pushForce, hitPointPos);

            // Print a message in Console saying that
            //the collision did happen and force was indeed applied
            Debug.Log("Detected hit with " + collisionTag +
              ", applying force of " + pushForce + " in " +
              hitPointPos + ".");
        }
    }
}
```

Press *command* + *S* (*Ctrl* + *S* in Windows), and let us look at what has changed apart from the things already mentioned. The syntax of the component requirement is different in C#. On top of that, the `RequireComponent` attribute has to be placed before the class declaration.

The `#pragma strict` directive is gone. C# is explicit by nature and requires that you specify types of everything, so it is not needed.

> In C#, the following are quite useful: `#region [Name]`/`#endregion`, which is a good way of dividing your code into regions that you can fold. For example, writing `#region Variables` will create a region called `Variables`. Then you will be able to press a minus in a rectangle on the left of the MonoDevelop window to fold the code region, the end of which you have to mark with `#endregion`.

The `function` keyword is not used. Instead, function declarations are preceded by return types. You can specify a return type in JS as well, but this is done with the `:` operator after the brackets, for example, `function Update() : void`.

Finally, all variable declarations are preceded with types of variables instead of the `var` keyword. There are more differences in syntax that we cannot see in this example because of the relative simplicity of our script, but these are the main ones.

Now, if you replace your JS script with the C# one on the Mallets, they will act exactly the same way as before. Try doing this, then remove the **Push Puck Action** component from the mallets. It is time to modify the script and transform `PushPuckAction.cs` into an actual Playmaker action. Replace the contents of `PushPuckAction.cs` with the following code:

```
using UnityEngine;
using System.Collections;

namespace HutongGames.PlayMaker.Actions
{
    [ActionCategory(ActionCategory.Character)]
```

```
  [Tooltip("Detect collision with CharacterController, then push
    the other object into the opposite direction.")]
  public class PushPuckAction : FsmStateAction
  {
    [Tooltip("Push magnitude")]
    public FsmFloat pushMag;

    [Tooltip("Object with this tag will be pushed")]
    public FsmString collisionTag;

    public override void Reset ()
    {
      pushMag = 20f;
      collisionTag = string.Empty;
    }

    public override void DoControllerColliderHit(
      ControllerColliderHit hit)
    {
      if (hit.gameObject.tag == collisionTag.Value)
      {
        FsmVector3 hitObjectPos = hit.transform.position;

        FsmVector3 hitPointPos = hit.point;

        FsmVector3 pushForce = (hitObjectPos.Value - hitPointPos.
          Value).normalized * pushMag.Value;

        hit.rigidbody.AddForceAtPosition(pushForce.Value,
          hitPointPos.Value);

        Debug.Log("Detected hit with " + collisionTag.Value +
          ", applying force of " + pushForce.Value + " in " +
          hitPointPos.Value + ".");
      }
    }
  }
}
```

Press *command* + *S* (*Ctrl* + *S* in Windows) to save the script. As you can see, this time more things have changed, although you can still see the same structure. Let us go through the code line-by-line and examine it.

Scripting and Custom Actions

The `using` directives are the same, but the difference begins right after them. The line `namespace HutongGames.PlayMaker.Actions` is obligatory for all Playmaker actions. Without it Playmaker will not know that the script that you are writing is, in fact, an action.

The `[ActionCategory(ActionCategory.Character)]` line puts your new action into a category. In this case, we are putting it into the `Character` category, because the action is about things colliding with the Character Controller. It could also go into the `Physics` category. To move it there, the line would have to be `[ActionCategory(ActionCategory.Physics)]`.

After that there is `[Tooltip("...")]`, which is quite self-explanatory. It shows a short description when you select the action from the list in the **Actions** panel.

The `PushPuckAction` class now inherits from `FsmStateAction` instead of `MonoBehavior`. You still have access to all the standard Unity classes, but Playmaker-specific ones are added now.

Then there is another `Tooltip`, this time for a variable rather that a whole action. The text within this tooltip will appear when you hover your mouse pointer over the variable in the **State** tab of the **playMaker** panel or in the **Actions** panel.

Note that the type of the `pushMag` variable has changed from `float` to `FsmFloat`, and the same goes for the `string` variable `collisionTag`—it is `FsmString` now. These are Playmaker types of variables. The same operations can be performed on them as before, but to access their value you now have to use the dot operator with the word `Value`, so, for example, `pushMag.Value` will return a float, the value of the Playmaker variable.

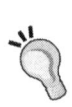

If you do not want to be able to assign a value directly in the **State** tab of the **playMaker** panel and force choosing from existing variables, you can write `[UIHint(UIHint.Variable)]` in the line before the variable declaration, the same way we did for the tooltips.

A `Reset` function was added. This is what happens when a new action is added to a state or when you right-click on the header of the action and press **Reset**. In it, we reinitialize the variables.

Then there is the `DoControllerColliderHit` function. Its name has changed from the standard Unity `OnControllerColliderHit`. Inside the function everything has stayed more or less the same with the only difference that types of `Vector3` variables have changed to `FsmVector3`, so to access their values `.Value` is used. Also, instead of `Vector3.Normalize`, we used `.nomalized`, which does exactly the same thing.

> While it is clear that in order to find examples and standard Unity classes' API one has to go to Unity Script Reference, it may be less clear about Playmaker-specific things. The easiest way to find examples is opening the script files of existing Playmaker actions that are located under the `PlayMaker/Actions` path, in your project. For example, if you are not quite sure how to detect mouse input and you want to do it via a Playmaker custom action, you can open `PlayMaker/Actions/MousePick.cs` and look at how the creators of Playmaker solved this problem.

Note that both `Reset` and `DoControllerColliderHit` have `override` preceding their types. This means that we are replacing a base function defined in the Playmaker with our own function. As a general rule, you will need to override all of the Playmaker standard functions using this keyword.

Now that we are done writing a custom Playmaker action, we can try using it. Remove the **Push Puck** and/or **Push Puck Action** components from **MalletLeft** and **MalletRight**. In their **Move** state, remove the **Collision Event** action. Then locate the newly created **Push Puck Action** in the **Actions** panel and add it to the state. Set the properties as shown in the following screenshot. Finally, delete the **Push Puck** state from the FSM as well as the **Push** event and transition. To delete a transition, you just need to right-click on the event in the FSM view and press **Delete Transition**.

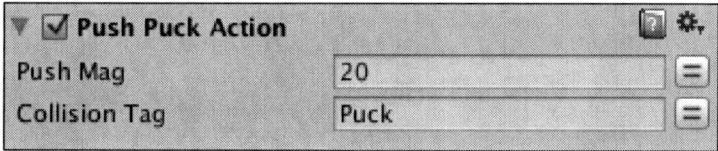

Summary

In this chapter, you were introduced to scripting in Unity, both JavaScript and C#, and learned how to create custom Playmaker actions. You should try repeating the process described in this chapter with another set of actions on your own. Set yourself a gameplay goal, for instance, you could take one of the exercises offered at the end of *Chapter 4, Creating Your First Game*, write a JS or C# script that accomplishes the goal; and then translate it into a Playmaker action. You will feel much more comfortable with scripting by the time you are done, as it is all about practice, and no amount of reading and theory can replace a hands-on experience with a text editor and a search engine.

The next chapters continue talking about advanced subjects, such as networking and external APIs, and we are going to do some more scripting in *Chapter 7, Working with External APIs*.

6
Networking and Multiplayer

In previous chapters you learned how to use Unity's interface, manipulate objects, and add components and behaviors to them. You created gameplay using Playmaker actions and Unity scripting. We also looked at making custom actions from C# scripts. You made a fully playable air hockey game with an AI opponent using all these tools.

In this chapter, we are going to talk about networking. You will make a multiplayer mode for the game using **Photon Unity Networking** (**PUN**), which is a helpful plugin that comes with Playmaker and lets you make multiplayer games almost effortlessly. We will also talk about the theory of networking in games and discuss Unity native networking as an alternative to Photon.

In this chapter, you will cover:

- Understanding networking and multiplayer
- Setting up Photon Unity Networking
- Making a multiplayer game

Understanding networking and multiplayer

Explaining things like TCP/IP and other low-level networking concepts is beyond the scope of this book, and we are going to try and keep everything as close to practical application as possible. On the other hand, it will be much easier for you to build multiplayer if you are familiar with at least some theory.

The first thing that you need to know is what servers and clients are. In simple terms, a server is a computer that responds to network requests from other computers, or more precisely, a system that responds to network requests from other systems, because you may have multiple servers and multiple clients on the same computer. This means that clients communicate with each other through a server. Typically, player systems are clients in multiplayer games, while servers are on computers that are accessed remotely. Sometimes, a player can *host* a game, in which case the player either acts as a server or simply tells the server to reserve its resources for the game.

You may have heard about network architectures before. In games, the most popular architectures are arguably client-server and peer-to-peer. The former means that all the clients subscribe to a single server. The server hosts most of the important information about the game and distributes it between the players. The latter is about peers (players) connecting to one another directly, so all the clients are connected to each other, and the network workload is distributed evenly.

The advantage of client-server is that it allows creating a more stable system that ensures that cheating is either impossible or very hard, as well as makes it easier for the developer to monitor everything and make changes to the game on the fly. This method, however, is generally expensive and relatively hard to implement yourself if you are just a solo developer who is learning to make his/her first multiplayer game.

Peer-to-peer does not require having a powerful server hosting multiple game sessions at the same time, allowing players to connect to each other, distributing the network workload between them. The drawback of peer-to-peer is that it tends to be less stable, and it is relatively hard to monitor. On top of that, you still need a server if you want to keep track of game sessions, perform matchmaking, and let your players play on the Internet instead of just a local network.

It is hard to connect to the Internet without having a server, because of something called **Native Address Translation** (**NAT**). Without getting into much detail, it should be noted that it is something that network routers do, and most of us have routers these days. A process commonly called **NAT punchthrough** is used in order to connect one computer to another, and this process requires a server acting as a mediator for the first connection between two computers.

In Unity, it is relatively easy to set up a **Local Area Network (LAN)**, peer-to-peer connection, or client-server connection with one of the players hosting the game without using any external plugins. A LAN connection means that all the players are connected to the same local computer network. Unfortunately, whatever you do, you will need a server to make sure that players can always connect to each other over the Internet, which is what we want to do. Photon takes client-server and wraps it in an extremely easy to use interface that allows anyone to create multiplayer games without any prior experience. On top of that, it is very affordable for what it is.

Some of the Photon services allow players to host their own servers, but those take some time to set up. What we are going to use in this book is Photon Cloud. As the name implies, all the game sessions happen in the cloud, thus on remote Photon servers. All you need to do is synchronize your game's data through them and make sure that players can find each other. You do not need to set up a server, and you do not have to worry about the problems involved in making peer-to-peer multiplayer.

The way the synchronization works is that there is something called **Network View** (**Photon View** in Photon), which is a component that makes one or more game object's properties synchronized over the network. When such a property changes in one client, it changes in all the clients, with the server keeping track of everything and sending commands to clients. For example, mallet's position can be such a property. This way, when player 1 moves their mallet, player 2 sees them move it and vice versa. The same goes for almost any other property.

As we will show in this chapter's example, synchronizing positions can be okay for player objects (such as mallets in air hockey or characters in first person shooters), but objects that have physical behaviors (such as the puck), can experience serious network delays on remote computers. There is currently no easy solution for this problem apart from using Unity native networking.

There are objects that can belong to the scene (like the walls and the background) and so are exactly the same and unchangeable throughout all clients, and then there are objects that belong to different clients, such as the mallets. Generally, you want to synchronize as little data over the network as possible in order to avoid high response times. Scene objects do not have to get synchronized since they do not change. Moreover, this way each player's mallet responds only to that player's input, which makes perfect sense gameplay-wise.

You are now ready to start setting up Photon. All this theory may sound complicated, but it really comes down to synchronizing variables over the network using a special Photon component called Photon View.

Setting up Photon Unity Networking

Photon Unity Networking is a free Unity plugin with an optional paid subscription that allows you to outsource most of the heavy lifting for building multiplayer games. The free version has full functionality but is limited by the number of players that can be online at the same time. This is not a problem, because all you need for testing is to be able to connect as many players as your game requires for being playable (so two for air hockey).

1. First of all, we will need to set up PUN. In the main menu, navigate to **PlayMaker | Addons | Photon Networking | Set up Photon Networking**. This should open the **Photon Setup Wizard** window. Click on the orange **Setup** button.

2. If this is the first time you are using Photon, you are going to need an account, so enter your e-mail in the appropriate field and click on the **Send** button.

3. After that you can finish the registration process by clicking on the link that you will have received by e-mail. Sign in to your account on `http://cloud.exitgames.com/`, click on the **New App** button on your account page, enter the game's name and description, and then click on **Create**. You should be redirected back to your account page. In the **Details** section, copy the code under **AppID** and go back to Unity.

4. In the **Photon Setup Wizard**, click on the **Setup** button, paste your AppID into the **Your AppId** text field, and choose your region by pressing one of the **Cloud Region** buttons. Make sure you choose the region that is closer to you geographically as this will affect the connection speed of your game's multiplayer.

5. Once you have pasted the AppID and chosen the region, click on the **Save** button below. A window should pop up saying that your settings have been saved. Click on **OK**. The following screenshot shows what the setup window is supposed to look like once you do:

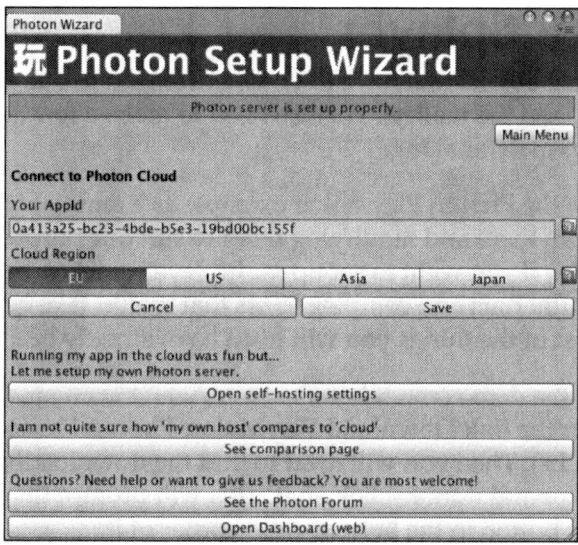

6. Make sure that the green label saying **Photon server is set up properly** appears near the top of the window. Press the **Main Menu** button right below it. It should take you back to the first screen of **Photon Setup Wizard**.

7. Make a copy of your main game scene and call it Multiplayer, load it by double-clicking it in the **Project** panel, and then go back to **Photon Setup Wizard** window and click on **Add Photon System to the scene**. The button should disappear, and you should see the second green label saying **The scene is set up properly**.

8. At this point Photon Cloud is set up, and you can feel free to close the wizard window. Save the **Multiplayer** scene, making sure that the **PlayMaker Photon Proxy** game object was added to **Hierarchy**.

You can modify the settings any time you want. You can also change your AppID if you choose to do so.

Now that we have added Photon to the project and made a scene dedicated to multiplayer, it is time to synchronize objects over the network and set up matchmaking.

Making multiplayer

There are a few game objects that have to be synchronized in our game, including the goals, the puck, and the mallets. We also need to make a few adjustments to the scene and set up matchmaking.

We are going to use the Photon Playmaker example as a template for our game, using the scenes from there and modifying them to suit our purposes. This is generally a good idea if you want to set up multiplayer quickly, because these examples feature numerous and complex FSMs that would take quite a lot of time to set up, while most of the things you will need have already been implemented.

You can download the demo scenes here: `http://www.hutonggames.com/samples.php`. Simply click on the link **Download PlayMaker Photon Demo** (requires Unity 3.5+ Playmaker 1.6.1+). Then you will need to find the downloaded `unitypackage` file on your computer and double-click on it. This will prompt the import window. Click on the **Import** button in the bottom-right corner of it.

> The warning on the example download page advises against importing the example into existing projects. We can ignore this warning, because none of our files are named in the same way the ones in the example are. As a general rule, you should always make sure that this is the case before importing new packages into new empty projects. Otherwise you might find yourself losing important assets in your projects.

Save the **Multiplayer** scene, and let us add the demo scenes to our project. They should be under `Photon Unity Networking/PlayMaker/Demo/Separated Scenes Demo`. Open the **demo_lobby** scene by double-clicking on its file.

The first thing we need to do is add the new scenes to our project. Open **Build Settings** by pressing *Shift + command + B* (*Shift + Ctrl + B* in Windows), then click on the **Add Current** button shown in the following screenshot. This will add the currently open scene to the project. Do this for **demo_lobby** and **demo_room**. Then close **Build Settings**.

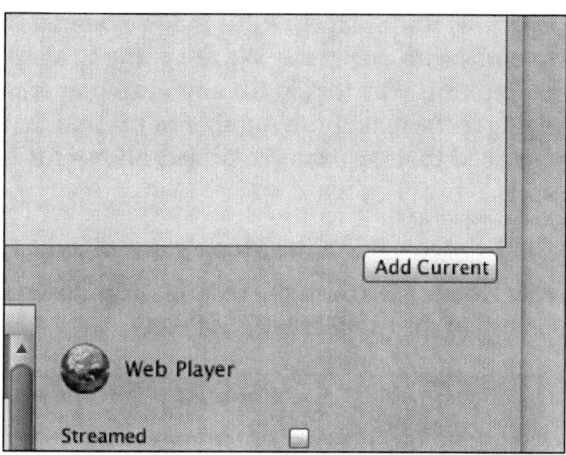

These two scenes are going to be responsible for two states of the game: the matchmaking state where players can find and create servers and the match state where the game itself takes place. You can test how it works by opening two instances of your game at once: one in the Unity Editor, one in your web browser.

1. To make a browser build, select **File | Build & Run** from the main menu and save the build files wherever you want on your computer when the file browser appears. You might want to create a special Build folder to make sure that you can always find your build. This should automatically open the game in your browser.

 Please note that your platform has to be set to Web Player as described in *Chapter 1, Getting Started with Unity and Playmaker*. If it is not, open **Build Settings**, select **Web Player** from the list on the left, and click on the **Switch Platform** button. Then close the **Build Settings** window.

2. Specify your nickname, and the name of the room next to **CREATE ROOM**, then click on **GO** on the right from the room name text field.
3. A new scene should load, where you control a construction worker that can walk around on a plane.
4. Keeping the game open in your web browser, go back to the Unity Editor; make sure that **demo_scene** is open and click on play.
5. Click on the **GO** button next to **EXISTING ROOMS**. This will join a random exiting room. Since we only created one room, both of the game instances will now be connected to the same game session. This way you can test how networking works by looking at your scene from the points of view of two players.

Networking and Multiplayer

Now that you have seen how multiplayer works in the example project, it is time to modify its scenes to work with our game. We are going to keep the matchmaking intact (in fact, it can be kept this way for almost any multiplayer game). The only thing that needs changing is the maximum number of players that can join a single room. You may have noticed that the example project allows for 100 players. We need to change it to 2.

1. In the **demo_lobby** scene, select the **Menu** game object.
2. Open the **Create Room** FSM from the second drop-down list from the left in the menu on top of the **playMaker** FSM view.

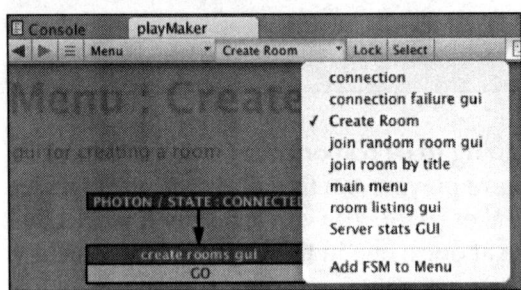

3. In the Photon Network **Create Room** action of the create room state, set the **Max Number Of Players** property to 2. Now up to two players will be able to join one room.
4. Save the scene.

Now that the lobby is all set, it is time to set up the game itself to work via the network.

1. Make a copy of the **demo_room** scene as backup to be able to go back to if something goes wrong. Open the original **demo_room** scene. You should have an unnamed game object with four children as well as **Chat**, **Game**, and the **PlayMaker Photon Proxy** game objects.
2. You can delete everything except the **Game** game object. This is where most of the initial multiplayer logic (such as instantiating players) takes place.
3. Save the scene and go back to the **Multiplayer** scene.
4. Select all the objects in this scene's **Hierarchy** by either pressing *command* + *A* (*Ctrl* + *A* in Windows) or clicking on the first item in the list and then *Shift*-clicking on the last one.
5. Copy the selected objects by pressing *command* + *C* (*Ctrl* + *C* in Windows), then open the **demo_room** scene again and press *command* + *V* (*Ctrl* + *V* in Windows) to paste them.

6. Create empty prefabs called `Goal`, `Mallet`, and `Puck` under **Prefabs/Resources**. Create the folders if you don't have them yet.

7. Drag the **GoalLeft** game object into the `Goal` prefab, **MalletLeft** game object into the `Mallet` prefab, and **Puck** game object into the `Puck` prefab.

8. Delete the following objects from the scene: **MalletLeft**, **MalletRight**, and **Puck**. They are going to be instantiated from prefabs that you just created when players join the room.

9. Make **GoalLeft** and **GoalRight** invisible by deactivating their **Mesh Renderer** components. These objects will be instantiated from prefabs as well, but not right away, so we need to keep them in the scene for their colliders to make sure that no mallets can get out of the table. You can also rename both of them `Blocker`, since they are needed to block the mallets.

10. Select the **Game** game object and open its **Game Manager** FSM in the **playMaker** panel.

11. In the **Variables** tab, make sure you have three **GameObject** variables: **goalRef**, **player prefab**, and **puck prefab**, as well as an **Int** variable **player count**. Drag the `Mallet` prefab into the **GameObject** slot of **player prefab** and the `Puck` into the the **GameObject** slot of **puck prefab**.

12. In the **Events** tab, create a new event called `Two Players`.

13. In the **Photon Network Instantiate** action of the **instantiate player** state, make sure that **Rotation** is set to (0, 0, 0).

14. Add another **Photon Network Instantiate** action to the same state. Set its **Game Object** property to **Goal** by dragging the `Goal` prefab from the **Project** panel. Set the **Position** property to (-7.98, 2, 0) and the **Rotation** property to (0, 90, 0). Set **Store Object** to **goalRef**.

15. Make a new state called `How many players?` and add **Photon Network Get Room Properties** and the **Int Compare** actions to it. Make sure the former is before the latter in the list. If an error saying that PlayMakerPhotonGameObjectProxy component is required appears, click on it, and the component in question will be added automatically.

16. Set the **Player Count** property of the **Photon Network Get Room Properties** action to the **player count** variable.

17. In the **Int Compare** action, set the **Integer 1** property to the **player count** variable and the **Integer 2** property to 2. Set **Equal** to **Two Players**. Check the **Every Frame** box. If you see an error about an event, ignore it for now; it will be fixed later on.

18. Make a new state called `Create Puck`.

19. Add a **FINISHED** event to the **instantiate player** state. Drag a transition from it to **How many players?**
20. Add a **Two Players** event to **How many players?** and drag a transition from it to **Create Puck**.
21. In the **Create Puck** state, add two actions: **Photon Network Instantiate** and **Set Position**. Make sure that **Set Position** is the last in the list. If an error saying that a PlayMakerPhotonGameObjectProxy component is required appears, click on it, and the component in question will be added automatically.
22. Set the **Game Object** property of **Photon Network Instantiate** to the Puck prefab variable. Set **Position** to (0, 0.3, 0) and **Rotation** to (0, 0, 0).
23. In the **Set Position** action, set **Game Object** to **Specify Game Object** and select the **goalRef** variable from the drop-down list. Make sure that **Vector** is **None**, **X** is 7.98, and **Y** and **Z** are **None**.
24. Save your scene.

This state machine is responsible for spawning objects that should be unique to different players: players' mallets and goals are spawned as soon as the players connect to the room, while the puck is spawned once the second player connects to make sure that player 1 does not win while alone in the room.

Now we are going to set the individual parameters and synchronization of each of the prefabs we created, starting with Goal.

1. Select the Goal prefab in the **Project** panel and add three components to it using the **Inspector** panel: **PlayMaker FSM (Script)**, **Photon View**, and **Play Maker Photon Game Object Proxy**. You can find these components by clicking on the **Add Component** button in **Inspector** and typing their names in the search field.
2. Drag the **Transform** component of Goal prefab into the **Photon View** component's **Observe** property.
3. Name the state machine ColorSync using the **FSM** tab of the **playMaker** panel.
4. Rename the starting state to is mine? and add two events to it: **YES** and **NO**.
5. Create two new states: **Green** and **Red**. Then make transitions from **YES** to **Green** and from **NO** to **Red**.
6. In the **is mine?** state, add a **Photon View Get Is Mine** action. Set **Is Mine Event** to YES and **Is Not Mine Event** to NO.

7. In the **Green** state, add a **Set Material** action. Set **Material** to the material you created for the green goal.
8. Do the same for the **Red** state, but choose the red material instead.

This state machine makes sure that goals change color in the beginning of the game. Verify that you still have the **PlayMaker Photon Proxy** game object in the scene. If you don't copy it from the **Multiplayer** scene. At this point you may want to build and launch two instances of the game to test that everything works well.

Now let us change the color of the mallets to match the goals' colors. We will also make sure that only the owner of the Mallet can move it.

1. Find the `Fsm Photon player` prefab under `Photon Unity Networking/PlayMaker/Demo/Resources` in the **Project** panel and select it.
2. Copy **Play Maker Photon Game Object Proxy** and the **Photon View** components over to the `Mallet` prefab by right-clicking the components' headers of `Fsm Photon player` and selecting **Copy Component** from the drop-down menu and then right-clicking one of the components' headers in the `Mallet` prefab and selecting **Paste Component As New** from the drop-down menu.
3. Do the same for three of the `Fsm Photon player` prefab's **Play Maker FSM** components: the ones called **GameObject naming**, **Position synch**, and **variable synch repository**.
4. Now the Mallet should have four FSMs. Rename the one called **FSM** to `Movement` to make sure we remember what it does.
5. Drag the **Play Maker FSM** called **variable synch repository** into the **Observe** slot of **Photon View**. Set the **Observe option** property to **Reliable Data Compressed**.
6. In the **playMaker** panel, open the **Movement** FSM and add a `Bool` variable to it called **isMine**.
7. Set up the FSM as shown in the following screenshot, making sure that both the **Move** and **Push Puck** states stay unchanged. If you don't have the **Push Puck** state (you probably have it) confirm that the **Move** state has the **Push Puck** action attached to it. In order to set a state as a start state, right click on it and select **Set as Start State** from the contextual menu.

8. Select the **Is mine?** state and add the **Photon View Get Is Mine** action to it. Set its parameters as shown in the following screenshot, then add a transition from the **Yes** event to the **Move** state:

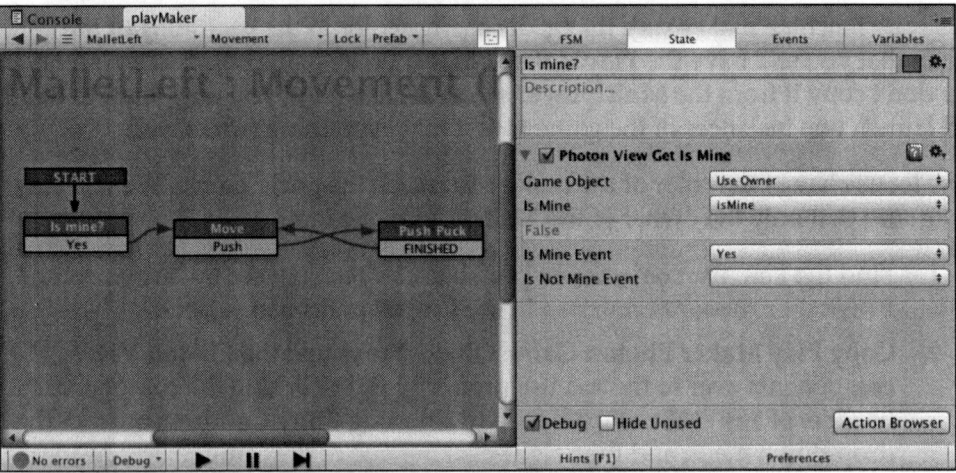

9. Switch to the **GameObject naming** FSM.
10. In the **add "me" to the gameObject name** state, add a **Set Material** action and set its **Material** property to the green material you created for one of the mallets. Don't worry if it is no longer green, just make sure that each player's **Goal** material matches his/her **Mallet** material.
11. In the **add player to gameObject name** state, add a **SetMaterial** action as well. This time set the **Material** property to the material that matches the red goal's material.
12. Switch to the **Position synch** FSM, and select the **Set player position with lerp** state.
13. In the **Set Position** action, set **X** to **None**, **Y** to `0.85`, and **Z** to **None**.

Now the mallets should be good to go, their positions synched over the network and colors set on startup. Save your scene and confirm that mallets' positions are synced by building the game and launching two instances of it while connecting to the same match.

All that is left is to sync the Puck's position over the network.

1. Select the `Puck` prefab and add the **Photon View** and **Play Maker Photon Game Object Proxy** components to it.
2. Copy the **Position synch** and **variable synch repository** FSMs to it from the `Fsm Photon player` prefab.

3. Drag the **variable synch repository** component of **Play Maker FSM** into the **Observe** slot of **Photon View** and set its **Observer** option to **Reliable Data Compressed**.
4. Switch to the **Position synch** FSM and select the **Set player position with lerp** state.
5. In the **Set Position** action, set **X** to **None**, **Y** to `0.3`, and **Z** to **None**.
6. Save your scene.

The last thing that you need to do is make sure that one of the players leaves the room instead of just reloading the level once the puck hits a goal. To do that, select the **GoalTriggerLeft** game object and, in the **LoadLevel** state of its FSM, replace the **Load Level** action with **Photon Network Leave Room**. Do the same for **GoalTriggerRight**.

Now your multiplayer should be set up. Before testing everything, confirm that you have copied all of the files over from the **Multiplayer** scene correctly. Make sure that there is a game object called **PlayMakerPhotonProxy** in both **demo_lobby** and **demo_room** scenes. If it is missing in one of the scenes, add it by going to **PlayMaker | Addons | Photon Networking | Components | Add Photon proxy to scene** from the main menu, then save the scene.

You can test it by making a build and opening it in your browser while launching the game in the Editor. Make sure you always start from the **demo_lobby** scene, because otherwise the matchmaking will not work.

You will see that the mallets' and the puck's positions are synched over the network. That is, they move simultaneously in both Editor and web browser. You will also notice that the movement of the remote object is somewhat jerky and imprecise (especially the puck on the host's client). This is due to the inevitable network delay and physics data being calculated more often than Photon packages are being sent. At the moment the only real solution to this problem is switching to Unity native networking, which, however, requires that you have your own server if you want the game to work over the Internet.

The place where the objects' movement is smoothed out is the **Position synch** FSM of `Puck` and `Mallet` prefabs. If you look at the **get player position** and **Set player position with lerp states** of these state machines, you will see that, if the object was first created on the local machine, its position gets saved in a variable every frame and synched over the network. If the object does not belong to the player's client, the variable is read, and then the position of the local copy of the object is interpolated.

>  You could try changing the **Amount** property of the **Vector3 Lerp 2** action in the **Set player position with lerp** state. This variable determines the precision of the interpolation. If you want to know more about the way PUN works under the hood, make sure you consult its online documentation that explains every state machine in the demo scenes in great detail: `https://hutonggames.fogbugz.com/default.asp?W927`

As you can see, Photon networking is quite easy to set up, but is not a very good solution for games that require physics simulation. This is mostly due to cloud server limitations and limited integration with the Unity engine. Most simple games that don't rely on physics so heavily can benefit from Photon greatly. In other cases, Unity native networking should be used. More information about it can be found in the Network Reference Guide section of the Unity documentation: `http://docs.unity3d.com/Documentation/Components/NetworkReferenceGuide.html`

Playmaker is capable of working with native Unity networking as well. You can check the **Network** section of the **Actions** panel for the list of available Playmaker actions and compare them with the actions described in the reference material.

Summary

In this chapter, you learned the basics of networking in games, set up the Photon Unity Networking plugin to work with Playmaker, and added PUN multiplayer to your game. We also examined the advantages and disadvantages of Photon and showed that it may not be suitable for physics games such as air hockey, because of the network delay.

The next chapter will show how to put your game on the Web and add Kongregate API to save game scores in an online leaderboard.

7
Working with External APIs

In previous chapters you created a multiplayer air hockey game. One way of expanding it would be making more levels and mechanics for it, but you already know how to do that. The other way would be integrating it with different external services, such as analytics, online scoring platforms, and leaderboards.

In this chapter we are going to talk about **application programming interfaces** (**APIs**). We will cover the following topics:

- API—what it is and what it's used for
- Existing useful external APIs
- The way Unity typically communicates with external APIs
- Integrating a game with one of the existing APIs (Kongregate)

We will look at some code snippets that you are going to use to integrate your game with Kongregate, test the game online, and save the number of times the player wins on Kongregate's servers.

About external application programming interfaces

In simple terms and in the context of Unity, an external API is an external library of code that can be accessed from a Unity script and provides some additional functionality to your game. Some APIs let you access the JavaScript code of the page your WebPlayer game is on, while others provide a possibility of transferring game data and getting information to remote servers.

You have already used one API in your air hockey game in the previous chapter: that of Photon Unity Networking. Most of the calls to remote servers are buried deep inside of its source code, but it is nevertheless an API.

Working with External APIs

Other APIs that you might encounter include online game platforms, such as Kongregate and Facebook; analytics tools, such as Google Analytics and Game Analytics; and online data storage platforms, such as Scoreoid and Steamworks.

In addition to different functions, APIs use different ways to connect to the external code base and different ways to communicate with it later, which may seem like a hard task, but rarely is. There is generally a comprehensive guide to the API on its website, and even when there is not the Unity community often comes to the rescue, putting together its own guides, template files, and code snippets readily available in Unity answers or forums.

We are going to integrate our game with Kongregate to show how this works and what kind of code you need to use. Kongregate was chosen as a fairly straightforward, very common, and completely free API.

Uploading your game to Kongregate

Before starting to use the Kongregate API, you have to see that you can actually upload your game to the website. To do that, you are going to need a Kongregate account if you do not have one yet.

1. Go to `http://kongregate.com` and near the top of the page find and click the **Register** link, as shown in the following screenshot:

2. A registration form should appear, offering you to either connect using Facebook or enter your account information manually. Do that and click on the **Sign Up** button.

3. Now, if you go to the Kongregate main page and hover over the **GAMES** button just under the sign-in block of the website, a submenu should appear, divided into three sections: **FEATURED**, **CATEGORIES**, and **DEVELOPERS**. It is the last one that is of interest to us. Find the **UPLOAD A GAME** button there and click on it.

4. Open Unity and make a Web build, like you did to test multiplayer in *Chapter 6, Networking and Multiplayer*; remember where you saved it.

5. On the Kongregate website, you now should have the game information menu. Enter the game's name, category, and description, then click on **Continue**.

6. The next step asks you to choose game files and upload them to Kongregate's server. Click on the **Choose File** button next to **Game File**, navigate to the folder where you saved your Web build from Unity, select the file with the `unity3d` extension, and click on **Open**.

7. In the two text fields below, enter the game's resolution (width 960 and height 600).

8. Upload an image as an icon. You can test, but cannot publish a game that does not have an icon.

9. You can also upload images as screenshots. This is not necessary, and you can do this later.

10. Check **This game is exclusive to Kongregate** if you are not planning to upload the game anywhere else. This will ensure that you get more ad profits for people playing your game.

11. Read the **License Agreement** and check the four checkboxes below it.

12. The **Statistics API** section is what we are going to be using the Kongregate API for. Click on **Add a statistic**.

13. Set **Statistic Name** to `Wins` and select the **Add Type** radio button. This is the statistic type, which determines how the statistic will behave. In our case, we will simply add the player's wins up. If your game had a scoring system, you could create another statistic of **Max** type for it.

14. Check **Display in leaderboards** to make sure that the statistic shows up on the game's public page.

15. Click on **Save**, then click on **Upload** on the bottom of the form.

16. After a short waiting period, the game should show up on your screen, being completely functionally playable. You can test the multiplayer mode to make sure that nothing has changed since you uploaded it to the server.

If everything works correctly, we should integrate our **Wins** parameter with the game itself. To do that, we will need to write a couple of scripts.

Writing Kongregate API code

There are two scripts that we are going to have to make in order to get our **Wins** scoring parameter saved and appearing in the leaderboards. The first one will set up Kongregate, make sure that the game is indeed on the Kongregate page, and inform the game about the API connection status.

Working with External APIs

The second script is going to be about incrementing a score for the player who wins based on the goal the puck hits.

Without any further delay, the following is the code for the handshake script, which is called `KongregateAPI`:

```
using UnityEngine;
using System.Collections;

// You have to add System in order to access the Convert class
using System;

public class KongregateAPI : MonoBehaviour
{
  // We are going to check this variable to confirm that
  // Kongregate connection is established
  public static bool isKongregate = false;

  // Player ID
  public static int userId;

  // Player account name. This can be used for greeting the player,
  // for example
  public static string userName;

  // Game ID
  public static string gameAuthToken;

  void Start()
  {
    // Establishing connection with Kongregate
    // Make sure that the game object this script is attached to
    // is in the first scene that gets loaded,
    // and that the name of the object it is attached to is
KongregateAPI
    Application.ExternalEval(
    "if(typeof(kongregateUnitySupport) != 'undefined'){" + "
      kongregateUnitySupport.initAPI('" + gameObject.name +
        "','OnKongregateAPILoaded');" + "};" );
  }

  // This method gets called if the game is on Kongregate
  void OnKongregateAPILoaded(string userInfoString)
  {
    Debug.Log("Kongregate connection established.");
```

```
        isKongregate = true;

        // Kongregate returns a string of chars that we divide
    and save into variables
        string[] parms = userInfoString.Split("|"[0]);
        userId = Convert.ToInt32(parms[0]);
        userName = parms[1];
        gameAuthToken = parms[2];
    }
}
```

This code is fairly straightforward and does not require much explanation on top of the comments already given within the script. Only two things should be noted: `Application.ExternalEval` is what makes your Unity game communicate with the JavaScript of the page it is on. Unity sends a message in the form of a string of text to the page, which is picked up by Kongregate and interpreted as code. The contents of this string are using the Kongregate API, the full version of which can be consulted here: http://www.kongregate.com/developer_center/docs/en/using-the-api-with-unity3d. `ExternalEval` is a very common method for accessing external APIs.

It is imperative that the game object your script is attached to (as well as the script itself) is called **KongregateAPI**. Create an empty game object in the **demo_lobby** scene and attach the script to it, then save the scene.

Once the JavaScript code on the page is executed, Kongregate sends a callback message back to Unity. This message always takes the form of the `OnKongregateAPILoaded(string userInfoString)` method. This, too, is part of the API. We then separate the string that it gives us using the | symbol and save parts of it into variables.

> There is really no point in making the Kongregate API script into a Playmaker action, unless you don't want to use any components other that Playmaker in your game, in which case I will leave it up to you to do it: the process is similar to that which we used in *Chapter 5, Scripting and Custom Actions*.

Working with External APIs

Unless you have changed something in the winning condition, the game does not currently distinguish between player 1 and 2 winning, and simply restarts the game no matter what happens. However, due to the fact that we have a multiplayer mode and want to save each player's wins, this does not work for us anymore. We are going to need to make the goal trigger into prefabs and spawn them the way we already spawn the goals and the mallets; then, when the puck hits one of them, detect if it belongs to us, and, if it does not, send the win to Kongregate.

To begin with, let us prepare a Playmaker action that sends wins to Kongregate.

```
using UnityEngine;
using System.Collections;

namespace HutongGames.PlayMaker.Actions
{
  [ActionCategory(ActionCategory.Level)]
  [Tooltip("Increment the Wins variable on Kongregate.")]
  public class KongregateSendAction : FsmStateAction
  {
    public override void OnEnter()
    {
      if (KongregateAPI.isKongregate)
        Application.ExternalCall("kongregate.stats.submit", "Wins", 1);
    }
  }
}
```

Here `Application.ExternalCall` is used. It calls an external function in the page as opposed to `ExternalEval`, which evaluates a code snippet that may or may not contain function calls.

> `ExternalCall` and `ExternalEval` both only work in Unity Webplayer.

Follow these steps in order to increment the **Wins** statistic on Kongregate:

1. Open the **demo_room** scene.
2. Create a prefab called `GoalTrigger`, then drag the **GoalTriggerLeft** game object to it from **Hierarchy**.
3. Delete both **GoalTriggerLeft** and **GoalTriggerRight** game objects from the scene; we are going to spawn them on startup.

4. Select the **Game** game object and, in its **Game Manager** FSM, add a **GameObject** variable called **goalTriggerRef**.

5. Navigate to this FSM's instantiate player state. Add a new **Photon Network Instantiate** action to this state. Set the **Game Object** property to **GoalTrigger**, **Position** to (-9, 0.42, 0), **Rotation** to (0, 90, 0), and **Store Object** to **goalTriggerRef**.

6. Open the **Create Puck** state and add a **Set Position** action to it. In this action, set the **Game Object** property to **Specify Game Object**, then set it to the **goalTriggerRef** variable. Set **Vector**, **Y**, and **Z** to **None** and **X** to 9.

7. Now that we have set up the instantiation of our goal triggers, we need to send our scores to Kongregate. Select the `GoalTrigger` prefab in the Project panel and add a **Photon View** component to it, then drag its **Transform** component into the **Observe** slot of **Photon View**.

8. Add a **PlayMaker Photon GameObject Proxy** component to the prefab.

9. In the **playMaker** panel, make the FSM look as shown in the following figure, adding all the missing states, events, and transitions.

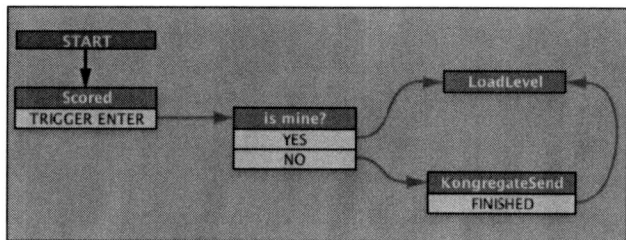

10. Add a **Photon View Get Is Mine** action to the **is mine?** state. Set **Is Mine Event** to **YES** and **Is Not Mine Event** to **NO**, provided that you have created the **YES** and **NO** events in the **Events** tab before. If you haven't, go ahead and do it now.

11. Add **Kongregate Send Action** to the **KongregateSend** state. This is the action that we created earlier.

12. Save the scene.

Now, if you build the game, upload it to Kongregate, play, and win, a score will be added. You should see a **HIGH SCORE** tab appear on the right on your game's page.

If it does not, don't worry, sometimes it can take some time for the first score to be submitted. If you feel like there is a problem, you can see exactly what commands Kongregate exchanges with your game by opening the JavaScript console of your internet browser while on the game's page.

Once you are sure that the game is working well and the **Wins** statistic is being submitted properly, you can either try adding some more stats or just publish the game by pressing the appropriate link near the top of the page. Then you can test it by either sending the public link to your friends or by opening it twice yourself and joining the same server.

Summary

In this chapter, you learned what an external API in Unity is and what kinds of external APIs there are, and then added one to your game. You uploaded your game to Kongregate and saved a game statistic for your multiplayer air hockey game on Kongregate's servers.

Index

Symbols

#pragma strict directive 78

A

Artificial Intelligence (AI)
  about 60
  implementing 60-66
Assets submenu 20
Asset Store
  URL 11
  used, for buying Playmaker 11, 12
Awake function 75

C

client-server networking 84
Code Academy
  URL 71
component
  about 36
  properties 38, 39
component-based architecture 35
Component submenu 20

D

default interface layout, Unity 14

E

Edit submenu 20
external application programming
    interfaces 97, 98

F

File submenu 20
Finite State Machine. *See* FSM
FixedUpdate function 76
FSM
  about 19, 43

G

game
  uploading, to Kongregate 98, 99
Game Analytics 98
GameObject submenu 20
game objects
  about 36, 37
  interactions 47-49
gizmo 30
Google Analytics 98

H

Help submenu 21
Hierarchy panel, Unity 23, 24
Hutong Games
  URL 11

I

Inspector panel, Unity 25-27
installation, Unity 8-10
interface, Playmaker 32-34
interface view 19

J

JavaScript (JS) 71

K

Kongregate
  game, uploading to 98, 99
  URL 98
  Wins statistic, incrementing on 102
Kongregate API code
  writing 100-103

L

Local Area Network (LAN) 85
low-level networking concepts 83-85

M

main menu 20
mallet
  moving 44-46
multiplayer
  about 83
  creating 88-96

N

Native Address Translation (NAT) 84
NAT punchthrough 84
Network View 85

O

OnControllerColliderHit function 74
OnDisable function 76
OnEnable function 76

P

peer-to-peer networking 84
Photon Unity Networking (PUN)
  about 83, 86
  setting up 86, 87
physics
  using 51-54
Playmaker
  about 11
  buying 12
  importing 12
  interface 32-34
Playmaker action
  script, transforming into 77-81
PlayMaker submenu 21
prefabs
  working with 39-42
project
  setting up 13-16
Project panel, Unity 28, 29
properties, component 38, 39

R

raycast 45

S

scenes 36
Scoreoid 98
script
  transforming, into Playmaker action 77-81
server 84
standard Unity classes
  overview 75, 76
Start function 75
state, FSM 43
Steamworks 98

U

Unity
  about 7
  default interface layout 14
  downloading 7
  Hierarchy panel 23, 24
  Inspector panel 25-27
  installing 8-10
  interface view 19
  main menu 20-22
  Project panel 28, 29
  URL, for downloading 7
  URL, for tutorial 71
Unity.exe 8
Unity.pkg 8

Unity script
  writing 71-75
Update function 76

V

vector geometry
  using 51-54
views, Unity 29-31

W

Window submenu 21
win/lose conditions 55-59
Wins statistic
  incrementing, on Kongregate 102, 103

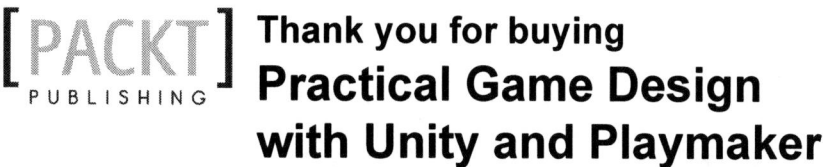

Thank you for buying
Practical Game Design with Unity and Playmaker

About Packt Publishing

Packt, pronounced 'packed', published its first book "*Mastering phpMyAdmin for Effective MySQL Management*" in April 2004 and subsequently continued to specialize in publishing highly focused books on specific technologies and solutions.

Our books and publications share the experiences of your fellow IT professionals in adapting and customizing today's systems, applications, and frameworks. Our solution based books give you the knowledge and power to customize the software and technologies you're using to get the job done. Packt books are more specific and less general than the IT books you have seen in the past. Our unique business model allows us to bring you more focused information, giving you more of what you need to know, and less of what you don't.

Packt is a modern, yet unique publishing company, which focuses on producing quality, cutting-edge books for communities of developers, administrators, and newbies alike. For more information, please visit our website: `www.packtpub.com`.

Writing for Packt

We welcome all inquiries from people who are interested in authoring. Book proposals should be sent to `author@packtpub.com`. If your book idea is still at an early stage and you would like to discuss it first before writing a formal book proposal, contact us; one of our commissioning editors will get in touch with you.

We're not just looking for published authors; if you have strong technical skills but no writing experience, our experienced editors can help you develop a writing career, or simply get some additional reward for your expertise.

Unity 4.x Cookbook

ISBN: 978-1-84969-042-3   Paperback: 386 pages

Over 100 recipes to spice up your Unity skills

1. A wide range of topics are covered, ranging in complexity, offering something for every Unity 4 game developer

2. Every recipe provides step-by-step instructions, followed by an explanation of how it all works, and alternative approaches or refinements

3. Book developed with the latest version of Unity (4.x)

Unity iOS Game Development Beginners Guide

ISBN: 978-1-84969-040-9   Paperback: 314 pages

Develop iOS games from concept to cash flow using Unity

1. Dive straight into game development with no previous Unity or iOS experience

2. Work through the entire lifecycle of developing games for iOS

3. Add multiplayer, input controls, debugging, in app, and micro payments to your game

Please check **www.PacktPub.com** for information on our titles

Unity for Architectural Visualization

ISBN: 978-1-78355-906-0 Paperback: 144 pages

Transform your architechtural design into an interactive real-time experience using Unity

1. Simple instructions to help you set up an interactive and real-time scene
2. Excellent tips on making your presentations attractive by creating interactive designs
3. Most important features of computer games covered, to develop compelling, interactive scenes for so-called "serious games

Unity 4.x Game AI Programming

ISBN: 978-1-84969-340-0 Paperback: 232 pages

Learn and implement game AI in Unity 3D with a lot of sample projects and next-generation techniques to use in your 3D projects

1. A practical guide with step-by-step instructions and example projects to learn Unity3D scripting
2. Learn pathfinding using A* algorithms as well as Unity3D pro features and navigation graphs
3. Implement finite state machines (FSMs), path following, and steering algorithms

Please check www.PacktPub.com for information on our titles

Lightning Source UK Ltd.
Milton Keynes UK
UKOW02f1254180214

226671UK00001B/81/P